INFORMATION INEQUALITY

THE DEEPENING SOCIAL CRISIS
IN AMERICA

Herbert I. Schiller

D0980474

ROUTLEDGE

New York · London

Published in 1996 by

Routledge
29 West 35th Street
New York, NY 10001

Published in Great Britain in 1996 by

Routledge
11 New Fetter Lane
London EC4P 4EE

An earlier version of chapter 4 appeared as "Media, Technology and the Market," in *Culture on the Brink*, ed. G. Bender and T. Drucker, Dia Center for the Arts, Bay Press, Seattle, WA, October 1994. An earlier version of chapter 7 appeared as "Transnational Media: Creating Consumers Worldwide," in the *Journal of International Affairs* 47:1 (Summer 1993). An earlier version of chapter 8 appeared as "Anticipating the Next Radical Moment: An Unanticipated Locale," in *Illuminating the Blindspots: Essays Honoring Dallas W. Symthe*, ed. Janet Wasko, Vincent Mosco, and Manjunath Pendkur (Norwood, NJ: Ablex, 1993).

Library of Congress Cataloging-in-Publication Data

Schiller, Herbert I., 1919–
    Information inequality — the deepening social crisis in America / Herbert I. Schiller.
      p.   cm.
    Includes index.
    ISBN 0-415-90764-0 (HB). — ISBN 0-415-90765-9 (pbk.)
    1. Information technology—United States. 2. Information superhighway—United States. 3. Distributive justice 4. Equality—United States. I. Title.
HC110.I55S35   1996
384'.0973—dc20   95–46613
                                                          CIP

INFORMATION INEQUALITY

By the Same Author

Mass Communications and American Empire
The Mind Managers
Communication and Cultural Domination
Who Knows: Information in the Age of the Fortune 500
Information and the Crisis Economy
Culture Inc.: The Corporate Takeover of Public Expression

Co-Authored

Hope and Folly: The United States and UNESCO, 1945–1985

Co-Edited

Superstate: Readings in the Military-Industrial Complex
National Sovereignty and International Communication
Beyond National Sovereignty: International Communication in the 1990s
Triumph of the Image: The Media's War in the Persian Gulf

For Lucy and Ethan

TABLE OF CONTENTS

ACKNOWLEDGMENTS

The many individual influences that shape a text are not easily traceable. Here I make a surely incomplete effort to acknowledge some of them.

I was fortunate to have the assistance of several talented (former) graduate students over the course of the book's germination and preparation. Helpful in numerous ways were Joyce Evans, Sarah Banet-Weiser, Jennifer Troutner, and Dennis Mazzocco. I am especially indebted to Judith Gregory, who contributed basic background research for the chapter on special effects.

As in the past, I relied heavily on my "information-rich" family infrastructure. Anita, Dan, and Zach Schiller and Susan Davis provided their considerable knowledge and encouragement to the work in progress. Edward Herman has been a steadfast friend.

Sandy Dijkstra offered good advice and solid support. Bill Germano was the initiating stimulus for the project. He has been a patient and understanding editor. Christine Cipriani guided the work to publication carefully and efficiently.

Hamid Mowlana at American University and Neil Postman at New York University provided me with comfortable accommodations and services while the project went forward.

In the end, however, this book could never have been completed without Anita's total dedication to my well-being and my recovery from an accident in the early winter of 1994.

INTRODUCTION

Inequality of access and impoverished content of information are deepening the already pervasive national social crisis. The ability to understand, much less overcome, increasingly critical national problems is thwarted, either by a growing flood of mind-numbing trivia and sensationalist material or by an absence of basic, contextualized social information. Consider:

Over a ten-day interval in the summer of 1994, the American media-cultural landscape was brightly illuminated by four separately reported press items: the announcement of the sale of a Hollywood film script; the auction of frequencies in the radio spectrum; an editorial on the leadership of American universities; and an advertisement listing jobs for a new category of academic professionals.

The first report described the record sale price—$4 million—for a movie script. It was noted that the writer had already distinguished himself as "a successful action writer." His new effort offers a woman assassin who "kills with her bare hands . . . corpses [are produced] every three or four pages of the script." This piece of writing was in great demand, the account indicated, because "the studios hunger for violent scripts, the bloodier the better. An action film release abroad can often double its revenue."[1]

A few days later, a much more substantial sale took place without any sign of overt mayhem. A portion of the public's airwaves (radio spectrum frequencies), hitherto inalienable, were auctioned off in a public sale. The highest bidders, not surprisingly, were a handful of the country's largest communications companies. Commenting on this sale, the telecommunications reporter for the *New York Times* wrote:

> Despite their value in whittling the Federal budget deficit, however, the auctions raise questions of whether contests of raw financial muscle are really the best way to manage the spectrum—a precious public resource that has always been viewed as having a social value beyond its economic worth . . . By any measure, this new embrace of market forces represents a fundamental break from past practice. . . . Last year, Congress authorized auctions amid a grow-

ing consensus that the "public interest" was so amorphous that marketplace
mechanisms were better suited to identify the best use of the airwaves."[2]

I will return to the "amorphousness" of the public interest, also understood
as the common good.

The third item, an op-ed *New York Times* column by the paper's educational writer, carried this headline: "At the Top of the Ivory Tower the
Watchword Is Silence." It detailed the remarkable reluctance of higher education's leaders to say anything of consequence about national issues.
Among the explanations offered for this "rhetorical tiptoeing through the
tulips" is the heavy administrative load of present-day educational leaders
and an unwillingness to rock the boat that is out in search of funds from
corporate and other wealthy potential donors.[3]

The fourth item may be considered a footnote to the above. An advertisement in the *Chronicle of Higher Education* announced the formation of a
"Division of University Relations and Development [and a] Department of
University Development." Given the current austerity in faculty hiring, the
number and character of the jobs being offered was astonishing. Eight new
positions were listed with the following job titles: Executive Director of Development; Director of Planned Giving; Director of Alumni Affairs and the
Annual Fund; Director of Major Gifts; Associate Director of Major Gifts—
2 positions; Development Associate; Records and Research Coordinator.[4]

What do these seemingly disparate reports have in common? Can four
unrelated press accounts sum up an era? Do they give full expression to the
essence of the age? Hardly. Still, they are markers of the current trajectory
of America's social condition as it moves closer to the twenty-first century.
They spotlight two powerful forces dominating the social sphere at this
time. These are a largely freewheeling corporate enterprise system, exerting
its will locally and globally, in tandem with an unprecedentedly influential
and privately-owned information apparatus, largely devoted to money-making and the avoidance of social criticism.

These are the primary sources of today's deepening social crisis, though
clearly other tributaries to current disorders also exist. Still, it is the corporate world's almost total rejection of social accountability, whatever the
arena, that produces a national mood of futility and a steady unravelling of
the social fabric.

How to explain this remarkable condition whereby the social needs of the
many are thwarted by the private interests of the relatively few? This would
not have been a noteworthy condition in an earlier time. Historically, a privileged few, with only the rarest exceptions, have exercised dominion over
the mass. But this is late-twentieth-century America. This is a country with
a long tradition of social struggle for the general betterment, and one in
which significant improvements have been achieved.

This is also a country with capacious message, image-making, and transmission facilities: thousands of magazines, newspapers, and radio and television stations, and millions of personal computers. So there is no lack of *channels*. It is the *content*, not the quantity, of instrumentation that is at issue.

There is, then, this puzzle. How can the business system act so cavalierly in a democratic society? And, no less puzzling, how can such a multilayered and substantial informational apparatus provide such a thin and restricted output of socially necessary images and messages? Developments over the past half century provide some clues.

The fifty years since the death of Franklin Delano Roosevelt have seen a sweeping shift in the exercise of power in the United States. It would, of course, be wildly inaccurate to conclude that preceding this period, a functioning democratic pluralism prevailed. Far from it! Roosevelt's indictment, for example, of the moneyed interest of his time may have been populist rhetoric, but it had a solid basis in the American political economy of the 1930s.

Yet in the pre–World War II years, there were some modest checks on what otherwise would have been the unbridled exercise of private economic power. A considerable organized-labor movement had come into existence. A crisis-stricken, but still articulate, agricultural population voiced its demands. Political office-holding was not yet the exclusive domain of wealth, or access to wealth. Presidential election campaigns did not require huge television outlays. Congressional and State offices also included many individuals representing the less favored sections of the population.

All this has changed. The corporate economy, which has grown tremendously in recent decades, now faces few, if any, *traditional* challengers. Domestically, its influence is evident in all realms. Congress's unwillingness, for example, to ban Big Business's hiring of workers to replace their striking employees permanently has, in effect, removed labor's historic and indispensable right to strike.[5] Without this capability, labor is literally at the mercy of its employer—a condition that has not existed since the early days of the industrial revolution.

Corporate authority over the workplace in the 1990s encounters few limits. To be sure, the workplace itself has changed greatly. A large proportion of production work has been transferred to low-wage areas outside the country. The work force in the service industries, excepting the public sector, is largely unorganized. The greatly increased number of technical and scientifically trained workers are permitted some latitude in their jobs, enough at least to encourage the (illusory) notion that they are not part of the capital-labor polarity.

Corporate influence is no less present—is actually more visible—in the political arena. It is exquisitely on display in the electoral process, where money rules. Here it is sufficient to signal the direction that this authority is taking. As independent voices in the national political theatre are eliminated or ignored, unabashed antidemocratic views and practices proliferate.

Increasingly, the voices that reach national audiences are those that secure the support *and the financing* of the moneyed crowd. Not surprisingly, therefore, a growing number of radio and television broadcasters, reviewers, and writers for the most influential papers and magazines, novels selected for the big promotions, films given the blockbuster production budgets, and social theories popularized in the media exhibit a marked preference for detailing the flaws, imperfections, and antisocial behavior of human beings.

A mean and dark view of human nature, one that emphasizes its rigidity and inherent defects, underpins a current unwillingness to entertain even minimally the prospect of social cooperation and human solidarity. Crime, delinquency, broken families, political and economic corruption—whatever the social ailment—are explained by pointing to *individual* weakness and inadequacy. Such a diagnosis conveniently removes malfunctioning institutions from scrutiny and discussion.

The disappearance from the world scene of a structured opposition to the global market economy also reinforces immeasurably the antisocial impulses being assiduously promoted. For the first time in almost a century, capitalism exists without powerful, organized opposition. As early as the second half of the nineteenth century, strong working-class movements developed in Europe, and later in the United States, offering and fighting for alternative roads to social development. In the twentieth century, revolutions installed nonmarket economies in several countries.

Flaws and weaknesses in these now mostly defunct regimes and movements notwithstanding, they constituted a century of pressure on the social orders in Europe and North America. This external force—mostly of example—along with growing domestic oppositional movements, contributed significantly to the lessening of exploitation and abuse in market-based societies. The emergence in the United States of a less cruel economic environment can be attributed to the power, not of an external aggressor, but to popular movements for social change, awakened and mobilized by alternative social visions.

Today, this pressure is virtually absent. Instead, the belief is cultivated that there can be no alternative to what exists. Herein lies the present strength of the U.S. "model," and, at the same time, its enormous vulnerability. While it is undeniably true that *at this historical moment* there is no visible opponent, or idea, that needs to be taken into account by America's political governing class, this condition feeds an already almost out of control exercise of private economic decision making. National governors, experiencing no apparent need to improve the general quality of life and lessen the glaring economic and social inequalities that are increasing across the nation, allow the already existing social fissures to deepen.

The satisfaction and complacency engendered by the smashing "victory" in the Cold War, and the consequent current absence of "foes," become, ultimately, sources of potential breakdown. It is remarkable, but not surprising, that the administrators of this demonstrably powerful society—"superpower" is its modest self-description—do not take the opportunity offered by their current preponderance to make changes that might extend systemic viability indefinitely. Yet long-term preservation, which could be facilitated by national initiatives for general social improvement, seems to be out of mind.

Instead, in a myopic pursuit of still greater private returns, the corporate-directed economy, methodically, is eliminating the institutions, structures, and the very idea of the public interest and the common good (which are, even now, seen as "amorphous"). The larger purpose, and its supporting practices, which hold the social enterprise together, are being down-sized. In the drive for private gain, functions that require and enlist the support of the full community are being privatized and stripped of their social character. Activities once community-based and identified as public are being detached from their social moorings and either turned into "profit centers," left without adequate maintenance, or eliminated.

Much of this demolition is done with the rationale of cost/benefit analysis. The costs for the services are calculated and matched against their purported benefits. Invariably, the benefits seem disproportionately low in comparison with the costs. This "finding" provides the go-ahead signal to the privatizers. The calculus, however, is brutally inapplicable. There is no quantifiably useful way of estimating the social benefit of publicly administered services. How, for example, can a price be put on the benefit of inoculating children against communicable disease? Who, other than system-serving economists, blinded by their formulas and lost in the market nexus, would dream of estimating the dollar value (benefits) of providing national child-care centers?

In truth, public services, by definition, mean everyone in the society benefits from their provision, often in indirect ways, totally outside the reach of calculation. Similarly, everyone suffers if these services are either limited to certain groups or denied altogether. When these services are stripped of their social character, privatized, and put on an individual ability-to-pay basis, the common good is grievously wounded. Along with the inevitable inequity that accompanies ability-to-pay standards comes a further weakening of the social organism. The more contractual arrangements enfold the lives of people, the less cohesiveness there is in the community.

In the United States of the 1990s, the notion of community has become mostly nostalgic. Every facet of living is being, or has been, transformed into a separate, paid-for transaction. This development is especially observable in the media/informational sphere, and is the focus of this book. Simply stated, the information crisis—denial of access and debased messages and images—deepens social inequality and intensify the general social crisis.

Today, the media/informational sector possesses extraordinary importance. It has become a major site of employment and income (domestic and international), and also provides an increasingly integrated symbolic environment from which the nation derives its ideas, values, and expectations. The capability of Americans to *begin* to undertake the far-reaching transformational tasks that are literally imperative to national sustainability depends to a very large extent on the adequacy and openness of the informational system.

The character and quality of the message and image flow, therefore, is a crucial terrain of contention in the time ahead. Cultural, media, and informational issues already are, and increasingly will be, centers of social dispute. This is as it should be. I would like to believe that this book may contribute modestly to the efforts of those engaged in current and future battles in defense of and for the revitalization and enhancement of the common good and its informational sustenance.

Notes

1. Bernard Weinraub, "A Script Strikes Gold: $4 Million," *New York Times*, July 25, 1994, sec. B, p. 1.
2. Edmund L. Andrews, "Airwaves Auction Brings $833 Million for U.S. Treasury," *New York Times*, July 30, 1994, p. 1
3. William H. Honan, "At the Top of the Ivory Tower the Watchword Is Silence," *New York Times*, July 24, 1994.
4. "Division of University Relations and Development: Department of University Development," advertisement by Cleveland State University, *Chronicle of Higher Education*, August 3, 1994, sec. B, p. 13.
5. James Risen, "Ban on Firing Strikers Blocked," *Los Angeles Times*, July 13, 1994, p. 1.

POLICING THE CULTURE

Policing The Culture

Why do we have such trust in, or perhaps cynicism about, the institutions and practices of American life that few question the structured positions of privilege and domination? This is not to say there is an absence of criticism of a social practice or an individual's behavior. Far from it! There is a surfeit of reports on misdemeanors and malfeasance, locally and nationally. Yet efforts to offer a comprehensive explanation of these varied examples of exploitation, corruption of office, and shockingly self-interested behavior of the well off and well positioned are invariably dismissed either as conspiratorial or paranoiac.

This has not always been the case. Often in American history turbulent social movements arose to challenge the order existing at the time. In mounting these sometimes large-scale protests, it was natural that many of the prevailing social institutions would be radically questioned.

Today, a remarkable edifice of invisible control has been constructed, permitting the most far-reaching measures of social domination to escape significant public attention. This achievement is all the more startling when it is accompanied by the bold assertion, widely believed, that the overarching condition of American life is freedom, freedom that exists throughout the political realm and encompasses the full range of individual behavior.

"Americans are free" is the message that circulates internationally. It is a statement that most Americans endorse. There are, of course, some who do not subscribe to this belief. For the most part, they are disenfranchised by color or income. It is a sizable group but is far from a majority.

Many elements contribute to the general willingness to accept the prevailing definition of freedom. Not least is the absence of easily identifiable controls over, and intrusions into, individual life. Actually, few *formal* censors preside over the public's reading, viewing, and listening habits and materials. With the same exceptions—color and income—there are no police visitations or harassments.

People can, with some exceptions, express themselves freely. Meetings and, to a somewhat lesser extent, parades, can be organized without difficulty. Macy's Thanksgiving Day Parade in New York City, televised nationally, has no trouble in getting a permit. Striking workers, however, might meet resistance in applying for a parade permit.

Where, then, is this invisible edifice of social control? Its central locus, to be sure, is embedded in the structure of the economy—the ownership of property and authority over the allocation of fundamental resources. Here, however, I will focus on another site of power, the cultural industries: film, television, radio, music, education, theme parks, publishing, and computerization. These industries constitute no secondary sphere of influence. Indeed, throughout the twentieth century, and especially during the last twenty-five years, the informational and cultural sector has ascended to a prominent place on the commanding heights of the economy. The term "cultural industries" itself is indicative of the fusing of cultural with industrial power.

More than in any earlier time, the cultural industries have assumed centrality in daily life and in the nation's overall economy. Consequently, the rules and procedures followed in these industries are, or should be, of vital interest. Found therein are the operational codes, appearing as unexceptional internal organizational practices, by which the outlook and beliefs of the community are produced, refined, and maintained.

The key lever at the disposal of cultural industry managers in regulating what people think and believe is the review and selection process. It is, in brief, the way cultural products and processes, are admitted or rejected for general public consumption. It includes also how individuals are selected for the many positions that need to be filled in the cultural industries (e.g., journalists, broadcasters, editors, administrators, teachers, curators, directors, and producers); in a word, how the cadres that work in the media and cultural spheres get their jobs.

Regis Debray, in his volume *Teachers, Writers, Celebrities*, had something to say about the review and selection process in the French context.

> The French intelligentsia applies the term [power] to the most varied collection of professional bodies, institutions and nouns, often pertinently, but never to itself. It never stops talking about the mechanisms, network and diagrams of the past and other places, but seems to maintain a stubborn silence as to its own mechanism of selection-censorship and promotion-exclusion *hic et nunc* in the university, publishing and media. Could it be that intellectual power does not exist in the eyes of the intellectuals?[1]

Reticence about this condition, applied to the cultural field, is no less evident in the United States. This is perhaps even more surprising since pop culture—the for-profit production of culture for huge consuming publics—has become a significant part of the domestic economy, while at the same time being a booming field of exports to the world market. It might seem that the breadth of this vast and constantly expanding sphere could not possibly be monitored. Nothing less than a huge administrative bureaucracy would be necessary to police the designs and contents of tens of thousands of media/cultural outputs, produced by a concentrated, but still considerable number of enterprises. Such an apparatus, even if successful—which is extremely doubtful—would surely defeat the system's claim of openness and freedom.

Actually, the supervisory task is handled much less intrusively and generally with little overt direction or publicity. Review and selection filters honeycomb the entire human developmental process, beginning with birth and early education, proceeding to job screening, and continuing throughout the individual's work career.[2] Rarely, if ever, is one in some locale that is insulated from invisible but omnipresent sorting, evaluative, and grading practices. Evidence of the totality of this phenomenon has been the appointment ordeals of several individuals proposed for high-ranking positions throughout the Clinton Administration. One candidate after another, presumably screened with some care to begin with, was abandoned when some detail from an earlier period of life surfaced and was viewed as problematic.

In one case, a sitting judge, Kimba Wood, was disqualified for a cabinet position because it was discovered that she had been employed by *Playboy* magazine for ten days when she was twenty-one years old. President Bill Clinton had to survive the damning indictment that he avoided participating in, and had protested against, America's involvement in the Vietnam War. On the other hand, Vice President Al Gore had the foresight to not get involved in student protests at Harvard. Mr. Gore "was in the class that disrupted the campus in April 1969, protesting the Vietnam War." He told the *Crimson*, Harvard's student newspaper, twenty-five years after the event, "that he had not taken part in that protest at the Dean's office."[3]

Few seem to think it unusual that every individual proposed for high, and sometimes not so high, governmental office—Supreme Court Justice, cabinet member, department head—must receive a security clearance before appointment. Yet what is the purpose of such a check? Is it likely that citizens who have had a long record of professional or business achievement are closet terrorists? Or, is this review only the final assurance that the candidate has, to that time, been distinguished by a lifelong unquestioning go-alongism—sometimes lauded as consensus-building? Yet such episodes of surveillance generally occur well along in an individual's career, if they occur at all. Well before government's, or business's, or the cultural industries' review and selection processes begin to be exercised, they are preceded by an initial far-reaching selection and instructional process. This is the basic education that each generation receives. How, to whom, and in what measure this education is provided, powerfully affects the outcomes of the later occupational sifting and screening. A very brief and broad-stroked consideration of the educational arena follows.

Educational Preparation: An Initial Screening Process

Selection begins with kindergarten, continues in the elementary levels, moves on through high school, and is especially pronounced for those in college and university and the smaller, though still substantial, contingent in graduate school. Along with screening there is the instruction, which when working well operates at all levels to produce acceptance and support of prevailing institutions and outlooks. An especially striking example of kindergarten selection is this account from Los Angeles:

> Next Tuesday, hundreds of parents of five-year olds will rush out to mail their applications to the John Thomas Dye School, a private elementary school in affluent west Los Angeles. The applications, for kindergarten classes beginning a year from now, must be postmarked on that day—no sooner, no later, no faxes. Many parents hedge their bets by applying to several [schools]. Some beg, some bribe, and some send reference letters from the likes of Mikhail S. Gorbachev, Vice President Al Gore, Gov. Pete Wilson and Supreme Court Justices. Some schools accept applications for newborns. One mother applied while in a hospital to give birth . . .[4]

The explanation for this frenzied behavior is affluent parents' efforts to provide their children with a leg up in the competitive schooling race. These mechanisms, however, are not always on automatic pilot and performing smoothly. Though the system is reasonably efficient in keeping those from poor households—which necessarily includes a considerable fraction of the minority population along with the white working class—from climbing into the privileged classrooms of the well off, it is not a rigid and total exclusion. Some do gain entry, though the general rationale that ability is genetic, along with the never-absent family income differential, serve nicely to exclude most of the poor and non-white youth from the advantages of a good education.

The content of the instruction also is not impervious to the economic and racial crisis overhanging the social order. Some educational efforts are made to ameliorate the near-breakdown of instruction in some of the poorer districts. Teachers, too, are not immune to the general social crisis. Some of them may try to address issues that are difficult to ignore. All of this produces effects that cannot easily be integrated into the control mechanisms.

Yet without significant change in job opportunity, income distribution, and concentrated property ownership, the educational (and general social) enterprise pitilessly creates and enforces the initial sorting-out process. At the same time, popular frustration and dissatisfaction mount ominously.

Meanwhile, the nation's schooling, with some exceptions, continues to stratify youth from childhood to maturity and to impart, also with exceptions, outlooks and beliefs that support rather than challenge basic institutions—the political process and the structure of the economy. Except for the elite and privileged universities, graduates are churned out who, for the most part, accept gratefully whatever jobs—if any—are offered to them. That satisfying work should be regarded as a human right seems to be an alien concept in America. But the United States holds no monopoly on this design. Among the conclusions from a study of French schooling, Pierre Bourdieu found "the illusion of the neutrality and independence of the school system with respect to class relations . . ."[5] That illusion is no less pervasive in the United States.

Class difference—never acknowledged as such, and explained, if at all, as income differentials—is the crucial economic factor that underlies the American educational enterprise, well before it launches its own stratification typologies. Children in the United States go to schools that are locally administered and locally funded. This decentralized arrangement may serve democratic goals but it also means that the neighborhoods that are affluent offer a level of instruction that is unavailable to poorer districts. As a result, quality and breadth of the teaching, along with material resources, differ widely from neighborhood to neighborhood.

Inequality of educational opportunity, based on income differentials between school districts, characterizes the country. In 1994, for example, "the poorest school districts in Michigan spent about $3,200 a student, and the richest, $10,000. In New York . . . the richest district spent nearly $46,000 per student, while New York City averaged $6,644 for each student."[6] Michigan and New York are among the richer states in the Union. A recent Harvard study on school desegregation found that the nation's schools "are now more segregated than they have been in twenty-five years. Sixty-six percent of black public-school students were in schools where enrollment was more than fifty percent black or Latino or both . . . Latino students were even more segregated, with seventy-three percent at schools that were predominantly nonwhite."[7]

This is the initial and deep divide that separates American children. It derives from the wildly unequal income that produces affluent white suburbs alongside impoverished urban neighborhoods. Its effects are carried over and intensified from one educational level to the next. In some instances there are redistributional efforts that attempt to level out somewhat the large financial differentials between communities. To date these have not come anywhere close to overcoming the existing huge resource gaps. The elementary school graduate carries forward to high school the advantages or disadvantages of his or her first educational experience. In most cases, these conditions will be reinforced, not diminished, because high schools are subject to the same determining forces affecting their instructional capability as elementary schools.

An account, tellingly titled "The ZIP-Code Route into UC" [UC is the nine-campus University of California], is illuminating, as well as descriptive of a country-wide condition:

> . . . a look at who is admitted to the prestigious University of California campuses shows that ZIP codes may be as critical as gradepoint averages in determining who gets in and who stays out . . . [They] reveal a system that favors the rich and the few. The list of feeder high schools that send more than 100 students each to UC reads like a social register . . . the UC feeders are in predominantly, if not exclusively, white, affluent enclaves . . . .

The report notes further that the opportunity to transfer to UC from a community college was originally intended to help those who could not initially make the grade. The community colleges were supposed to open up opportunity to those who, for a variety of reasons, started with disadvantages. The report finds:

> . . . to the extent that transfer from a community college to UC works at all, it works primarily for the select, the affluent—and principally the white—community college. The top ten community college feeder campuses to UC for fall, 1986, were mainly in affluent residential communities: Santa Monica, Diablo Valley, Santa Barbara, Orange Coast, Cabrillo, El Camino, De Anza, San Diego Mesa, American River and Saddleback. . . . For community colleges with heavy African-American and Latino enrollments, transfers to UC were minimal.[8]

The community college system itself has been transformed and now serves as an important screening agent, channelling most of its students into vocational education and away from seeking access to a general university education. This was not the original intention of the community college, as Steven Brint and Jerome Karabel make clear in their book *The Diverted Dream*.[9] Initially, the community college was developed to offer mobility to those students who had been barred, one way or another, by ethnicity, race, and income from receiving a college education. The community college was to provide a preparatory and transfer route for those who otherwise would have missed out. This "dream" was diverted in the 1970s, according to the authors, into what is now mostly a vocational education. As nearly five million students are enrolled in community colleges nationwide, this is no minor diversion. One reviewer of Brint and Karabel's book got the message: "For the working class and minority students that predominate in two-year institutions, this book serves as a cruel reminder of the limits of opportunity in a class-structured society."[10]

American education is no sealed hierarchical system. Alongside income, race, and geographic barriers (rural households), considerable movement occurs. There are scholarships. Capability may be recognized. Many teachers are dedicated and do the best they can to overcome structural realities. All this notwithstanding, the total educational edifice, from bottom to top, acts as a powerful sorter and grader of each generation.

Those who are chosen to fill the key jobs in the economy come, not exclusively, but heavily, from the "quality" schools. A reviewer of a study of elite schools, reaches these conclusions: ". . . there is indeed a 'high-status track' of elite institutions disproportionately attended by the already advantaged and disproportionately enhancing the opportunities for success of those most highly endowed."[11] This is academese for stating that students from high-income families get into the elite schools, go to a few dozen prestigious universities, and wind up with the best and most powerful jobs in the economy. This progression, which repeats itself from generation to generation, is the foundation of, and the starting point, for our analysis of the cultural industries' review and selection process. Account must be taken of wide differences between one cultural sphere and another, and the specific experience of individuals. But the general applicability of the process, and the validity of the foundation, will be evident in what follows.

Review and Selection in the Cultural Industries: Publishing and the Press

If class origins have an inordinate influence on the amount and quality of an individual's schooling, which dramatically affects employment opportunities, a second powerful systemic force comes into play after employment begins. Most jobs in the cultural industries today are with corporations that preside over vast chunks of the production and distribution of cultural outputs. Though there are tens of thousands of independent or freelance writers, filmmakers, video producers, photographers, musicians, dancers, and actors, the bulk of the cultural work provided to the American public is organized and controlled by a handful of giant businesses.

Ben Bagdikian published the first edition of his book *The Media Monopoly* in 1983. In the fourth edition, in 1992, he wrote:

> With each subsequent edition of this book, concentration of control over our mass media has intensified. Ownership of most of the major media has been

consolidated in fewer and fewer corporate hands, from fifty national and multinational corporations at the time of the first edition to twenty with this fourth edition. Although there are sometimes hundreds or thousands of small firms sharing the market that remains, the power of these scattered smaller firms is negligible. They operate in a world shaped by the giants. For example, there are more than 3,000 publishers of books, but five produce most of the revenue.[12]

Elite control of the "high" arts—classical music, ballet, dance, painting, sculpture, and architecture—has long existed in America. Moneyed folk supported these fields and their preferences dominated. Cultural product for the majority of Americans—film, TV, sports, pop music—was managed as business enterprise early on. In the 1990s, such distinctions no longer apply. Practically all cultural output—high-, middle-, and low-brow—is corporate. Elite domination of high art has shifted to corporate control "without seriously challenging [class] domination itself," notes one sociological study. In fact, this development, the authors observe, has "heightened concern with content and emphasis on the legitimating role."[13]

What corporate domination of culture means is that those who get jobs in the varied cultural fields are subject, in different measure, to the commanding logic of corporate business. This logic, as will be evident in the many examples that follow, insists on the unquestioned priority of extracting the largest profit possible from the specific cultural product. It should provide as well, unless it interferes with profitability, ideological comfort and support to the prevailing social order. These are the working instructions, hardly necessary to be put into manuals, for the employee cohorts of the cultural industries. Employees, whatever their rank and status, disregard them at the cost of their job security.

The adoption of these criteria to American book publishing is especially disturbing, if not ironic. Many of the liberal arts and humanities graduates of the privileged schools and colleges in the past found their careers in publishing. Here they became the readers, editors, and sometimes publishers of the books that supplied the country's cultural ambience. Publishing long prided itself, not necessarily with justification, as separate from the crass commercialism of the rest of the economy. High standards, individual taste that accommodated talent which may not have been mainstream, and personal relationships between writers and editors were said to be the characteristics of the trade. Whether, in fact, these conditions were as widespread as claimed, they are increasingly difficult to locate in today's publishing industry.

A few big firms dominate the industry. Reinforcing their own corporate inclination to emphasize the publication of works that promise large sales are the bookstore chains. These retail outlets, numbering in the thousands and accounting for half of all book sales, are owned by only three companies. They add their considerable pressure to the same objective that moves the publishers: maximizing sales. "The chains' power is exerted quietly every day," one reporter notes, "as they decide which books to carry. With the huge orders that they place with publishers, and with their enormous promotional budgets, the chains' decisions help assure that some works will be best sellers while others are consigned to obscurity."[14]

As corporate concentration in publishing and sales (distribution) grows larger, the space for a free marketplace of ideas narrows. Not only is the selection process for publishable manuscripts constricted by the preponderance of power of a few selectors, once the publishing decision has been made, the ample resources of the publishers and chain book stores are employed to publicize and promote the work. Radio interviews, TV appearances, and personal book signing tours are arranged for the prospective big sellers.

The biggest promotional force of all is advertising. This is carried out mostly in newspapers and magazines, though more and more, for the expected blockbusters, on television. Advertising publicizes the appearance of the book and provides a second, less-acknowledged benefit to the advertiser/publisher. It makes it far more likely that the book will be reviewed in the essential review publications: the *New York Times Book Review*; other major newspaper review sections; a few important review periodicals such as the *New York Review of Books*; and now, most importantly, talk shows on radio and television. The connection between the advertising expenditure and the publication of a review is quid pro quo. Each year more than 50,000 books are published in the United States. The Sunday *New York Times Book Review*, nationally distributed and the single most influential review source in the country, may publish 1,200 reviews in a year. Though it is not the sole consideration, the advertising budget a publisher devotes to the *Book Review* cannot avoid making an impression on the editor choosing which books to review. There may not be a one-to-one relationship involving one book and its specific advertising budget, but the yearly advertising expenditure by the publisher in the *New York Times* can only be disregarded at the magazine's financial peril. No editor can be oblivious to such an economic fact of life. The evidence that supports this contention is provided weekly in the *Book Review* (or any other national review channel). Count the number of times that a university press (tiny advertiser) book is reviewed. Note the publishers' names of the books that are reviewed. Invariably they are the big spenders on promotional copy. Finally, look for mention of works that are published by alternative or critical houses. Occasionally one may be found. (The word "occasionally" may be overly generous.)

After a book is selected—already an achievement—the assignment of a reviewer is the next critical step in the sifting process. Here the process becomes almost opaque. Always there is the assurance that the selection of the reviewer is "even-handed," fairly, if not objectively, arrived at, and justified by the selectee's expertise. These guarantees should be weighed alongside the underlying structural conditions already examined; the social backgrounds of the industry's employees, the criteria of the cultural corporation's management, and, not least, the general insecurity that characterizes capitalist employment overall.

Writing in the *Columbia Journalism Review* about the book review process, Steve Weinberg asserts that "almost every author, agent, editor, and publisher in the country has a conspiracy theory about the *New York Times'* reviews—and Book Review editor [at the time] Rebecca Pepper Sinkler says she spends an enormous amount of time trying to explain there is no conspiracy."[15] There is no need for a conspiracy theory to explain what goes on either in the *Times'Book Review* or other leading reviews. When the key editors themselves have been carefully chosen, it is not likely that their assignment of individuals to review newly published work is going to upset mainstream thinking. As hundreds of such choices are made in a year, there is some room for variability and even unexpected outcomes. But in general, and over time, the choices of reviewers and what their commentary will be, are fairly predictable.

In areas where the potential for controversy is relatively limited, some imagination and openness in the choice of reviewers are readily tolerated. Toleration quickly diminishes when the subject matter concerns issues that are socially significant. In fact, books that approach social questions from a critical standpoint are rarely selected for review. A review, for example, of a Monthly Review or South End Press book in the *Times Book Review*—or in other commercial media for that matter—would be an event calling for champagne. What the review would be likely to say, however, might make the author spill that drink.

What constitutes a "controversial book" is itself a controversial question. With the American political spectrum in the mid-'90s no longer containing a discernible leftist pole, the task of defining what is controversial has been taken over by conservatives. Under these stewards, a book or an idea is controversial if it moves further *right* than their currently dominant sentiments. Accordingly, it is controversial to argue that African Americans are genetically inferior but it is entirely acceptable to make this assertion and have it considered as proper terrain for "reasoned" discussion. The massive attention in the print and television media accorded the book by Charles Murray and Richard Herrnstein, *The Bell Curve*, an unabashed effort to demonstrate the genetic inferiority of African Americans, is one example of this current definition of controversial.[16] It is in this bizarre (at least to some) context that a reporter in *Publishers Weekly*, the weekly voice of the publishing industry, can write that a right-wing volume, *Illiberal Education,* is sure to be controversial, a prospect that makes every publisher's heart leap." Perhaps! But publishers' hearts can be heard faintly, if at all, if the manuscript before them comes from a social critic on the Left.

Jon Wiener discussed the fate of a few genuinely controversial manuscripts in a *Nation* article entitled "Murdered Ink." Wiener gave this neat precis of the book-review process:

> There are many ways to kill a book, as anyone who has worked in publishing knows. Manuscripts can be rejected at a number of points before their final delivery. Less frequently, manuscripts that have been copy-edited and announced in the publisher's catalogue can be yanked almost literally from the presses. Then there's the publishing industry's death-in-life, books that are printed rather than published, sent out into the world with tiny press runs and no advertising. (And of course, as Andre Schiffrin, director of The New Press, reminds us,) there are also the worthy books that don't get killed but are never born because they are never signed up to begin with.[17]

Wiener's article focused on another mode of book destruction, books killed by the publisher *after* they were written, sometimes actually printed. This occurred because their contents offended powerful individuals or companies. Included in Wiener's admittedly incomplete account were volumes on Disney, Paramount Communications, the owners of Jordache Jeans, and the coup in Chile.

Such examples are legion but difficult to identify for obvious reasons—the rejected author has no platform from which to complain. Suggestive, however, of this fairly common plight, is an unusual book review in the *Los Angeles Times*, of an author's self-published volume. The reviewer wrote: "Even Shannon [the author] a San Pedro native who had three novels published in England, couldn't find a major publisher for [his book] despite its thoughtfulness, its wit, its well-rounded characters and its lean, readable prose." Perhaps the fact that the book's subject was about "three generations of left-wing activists" and "the drying up of radical politics in the United States" explains its rough course to publication.[18]

Book publishing and book reviewing are complex activities. Here we have touched only on a few of the many means and techniques that determine whether or not a book will receive the public's attention. Why certain genres are supported extravagantly by publishers and others languish are, almost without exception, market-driven outcomes. In short, commercial publishing is a profit-seeking industry.

One sphere of the industry that cannot be considered here, but must be mentioned, is textbook publishing. Textbooks directly influence their readers—children, adolescents, and young adults—and serve as initial and life-long markers for the values and beliefs of those who are compelled to read them. The selection process for textbook publishing is affected by many forces—parents, state review boards, groups with strong opinions on social development issues, and so on. Yet in this sphere, too, the publishers' concern for profitability is the overriding factor. What will be included, excluded, how lengthy the text, and the level of the book's language are less pedagogical considerations than they are marketing and ideological concerns.

The Press and Its Review and Selection Processes

Decades ago, Warren Breed wrote about "social control" in the news-room.[19] He discussed the processes by which journalists were made to conform to prevailing codes, conventions and the dominant mind-set of the enterprise. Newsrooms today are dramatically different than those that Breed was examining. Computerization and digitalization have totally changed news reporting, editing, and printing. But new technology notwithstanding, two enduring structural features continue to play decisive roles in the selection and performance of present day journalists. One is the continuing concentration in the ownership and control of the nation's press and what that has led to. The other is the selection and training of journalists.

Ben Bagdikian reports that although there are 1,600 newspapers in the United States, "fourteen dominant companies have more than half of the daily newspaper business."[20] Most American cities are now one-newspaper towns, served by a single monopoly paper, generally a chain-owned product. The Gannett chain, for example, owns ninety-three papers across the country, and in most places, theirs is the sole paper in the community. Concentrated media ownership nationally and locally constitutes the work environment of journalists in the 1990s. These are conditions hardly conducive to independent, freewheeling, critical journalism. Previously, a strong union might have protected journalists from owner coercion. But the effects of continuous mergers and the general antilabor atmosphere of recent years have weakened this bulwark of journalistic autonomy.

Structurally, the newspaper industry is now more than ever a corporate employer. Its products are news and entertainment, *as it defines these categories.* Most journalists either work within these defining boundaries or move out of the industry. The effect of this on the journalistic "product" is set forth in a recently published book aptly titled: *Market-Driven Journalism.* John McManus, its author, concludes:

> ... the effort undertaken to satisfy the audience, whether in broadcast or print, is not democracy of the one-person-one-vote variety. Market journalism values the attention of the wealthy and young over the poor and old because news selection must satisfy advertisers' preferences. In fact, rational market journalism

must serve the market for investors, advertisers, and powerful sources before—and often at the expense of—the public market for readers and viewers. To think of it [market-driven journalism] as truly reader- or viewer-driven is naive . . . . Most of the time market journalism is an oxymoron, a contradiction in terms.[21]

McManus' conclusion is confirmed time and again. It was the subject of a book by James D. Squires, former editor of the *Chicago Tribune*: *Read All About It! The Corporate Takeover of America's Newspapers.*

Yet for most journalists these boundaries are not characterized as limiting. Many, if not most, journalists would wonder why anyone would regard the present industry structure as personally confining. This dichotomy has its explanation in the education and training of journalists. In the early days of newspaper reporting, most reporters generally received their training after they were hired. Some still do. But the large majority of new hires today, in print and broadcast journalism, come with a degree from an accredited school of journalism, generally a unit in a university. One estimate in 1988, claimed that "roughly eighty-five percent of entry-level print journalists are journalism school graduates.[22]

The journalism student, one of almost 90,000 aspirants, already screened by innumerable filters in the educational process, receives another submersion in dominant perspectives along with the techniques to ply the trade. Journalism school faculty are, mostly, former journalists themselves, often alumni of the school in which they are now employed. The prestigious journalism schools—whose graduates occupy important slots in the profession—boast about the student-faculty-job relationship that is as close to self-reproduction as they can make it.

A Gannett Center report, published in its own *Journal*, carried an article on "Eleven Exemplary Journalism Schools" which, when examined closely, means institutions that employ former influential journalists who have the connections to secure good jobs for their students.

Northwestern's Medill School of Journalism is described thusly: "The school attracts exceptional professionals to its faculty, most of them alumni. Medill alumni are everywhere, and in high places." Minnesota's journalism school is found to be "well-funded from private sources, [which is] a sign of the respect it has earned from the press of its region." Missouri's highly regarded school's "historical strength comes through in the 'Missouri Mafia' of well-placed professional journalists who look kindly on newly-minted fellow alumni." Other schools received similar stamps of approval from the report: Illinois, Indiana, Syracuse, Maryland, North Carolina, Florida, Texas, and Stanford.

Surprisingly, Columbia University's graduate school of journalism gets a poor grade, presumably because "The students are attracted by its reputation and by the perceived contacts and job opportunities they will receive after graduation. But those benefits don't exist as they once did." Self-contained and self-reproducing as they are, there is a certain administrative unease about *some* features of the schools' structures. A "shocking shortage of women faculty and administrators," and "a serious shortage of black and other minority students and faculty" are acknowledged.[23]

Actually, these conditions are not looked upon complacently in a good part of the industry. Whether defensively or out of conviction, at least limited efforts have been made and steps taken—in many media enterprises—to change these patterns.

It is an entirely different matter, however, when the question of the guiding philosophy and the principles of professional journalism are concerned. On these issues there is no room for discussion, much less change, in the dominant perspectives and the operating practices they underpin.

The foundation of American press freedom, a *privately-owned* press, or radio, or TV station, is sacrosanct terrain. The matter-of-fact and unquestioned connection of press freedom to financial support from advertising constitutes the other pillar of the journalistic enterprise. Not surprisingly, in many journalism schools and colleges of communication, journalism and advertising and public relations departments or programs coexist, if not happily, at least pragmatically. If for no other reason than proximity, most graduates of journalism schools find nothing remiss with a curriculum that embraces advertising, public relations, and journalism. It is the *normal* way of looking at the field.

It is illuminating to read the explanations of conservative writer Dinesh D'Souza for what he finds is a "left-liberal worldview" of TV journalists. Leaving aside, for the moment, the contradictory belief that journalists who accept without question the basic principles of press freedom can be considered "left-liberal," D'Souza's ruminations on how journalists' outlooks are formed are perceptive and entirely credible:

> No matter where he comes from the aspiring TV [the same holds for print press] journalist typically adopts a left-liberal world view as he picks up the tools of the trade. There is nothing conspiratorial in this. To get their stories on the air, TV journalists have to embrace the culture of network news, either consciously or unconsciously. It is only natural that an ambitious, social climbing reporter from the heartland who wants to please his colleagues and his superiors will absorb their ideas of what makes a good story, of what is considered responsible journalism. And since the culture of television journalism is liberal, it is hardly surprising that reporters get their idea of what is news—ultimately the most ideological question in journalism—from a whole range of left-liberal assumptions, inclinations, and expectations. It is very difficult for them to recognize the social and cultural forces that have shaped their work, not only their conclusions but also their assumptions.[24]

Substituting "typical journalist" for the "left-liberal" typology that D'Souza sees as pervasive provides as good a description as one could ask for to explain how journalists develop their mind-set. A summary glance at American journalism as it is practiced in reality, at once confirms D'Souza's view of the socialization process for journalists, while at the same time it negates his belief that left-liberalism is its dominant outlook.

Here, the studies of the nonprofit media research organization, Fairness and Accuracy in Reporting, FAIR, provide an empirical basis for judgement. Two 1989 FAIR reports give a picture of American TV journalism that is irreconcilable with the notion that there is a liberal/leftist bias in reporting. In one report, "Are You On the *Nightline* Guest List?", forty months of *Nightline* programming, from January 1, 1985, to April 30, 1988, was monitored. This widely-viewed current affairs and interview show hosted by Ted Koppel has an influence on the political thinking of Americans that certainly cannot be quantified, but it is one of the most highly rated and regularly watched programs in the country.

What were the findings of the FAIR reports? Excluding the network's own correspondents or analysts, five invited guests appeared more than ten times. They were: Henry Kissinger (fourteen appearances); Alexander Haig (fourteen); Elliott Abrams (twelve); Jerry Falwell (twelve); and Alejandro Bendana (eleven). The study states that "the four most frequent guests [were] either staunch cold warriors or rightwing ideologues, or both." Other breakdowns reveal similar one-sidedness in the heavy representation of the nation's elites and status quo-supporting speakers. "On the whole," the report concludes, "*Nightline* serves as an electronic soapbox from which white, male, elite representatives of the status quo can present their case. Minorities, women, and those with challenging views are generally excluded."[25]

A second study, by the same authors, also under FAIR's auspices, was conducted in 1989. It reviewed and examined the guests on the *McNeil/ Lehrer NewsHour* from February 6, 1989, to August 4, 1989. *McNeil/Lehrer*, the nightly news show of the public broadcasting service, allows much more time for extensive commentary and interviewing than do the major networks' nightly news programs. Also, public broadcasting still conveys, no longer justifiably, a noncommercial, nonpartisan image. For these reasons, *McNeil/Lehrer*, watched mostly by upscale viewers, presents itself as a reasoned, balanced, and honest inquiry of the domestic and foreign issues of the day. It avoids shrillness and exudes integrity. Is this image sustained by the diversity of its guests? The later FAIR study concludes:

> In the end, this supplement to our original *Nightline* study reaffirms the key findings of our first report. Both *MacNeil/Lehrer* and *Nightline* fall far short of

being politically or socially inclusive. Their limited political scope generally excludes critics in favor of voices of the powerful. Conservative advocates regularly appear as "experts," while progressives are identified as partisans. And foreign policy debates are almost the exclusive property of policy makers.

The study also found that

> a total of eighty-nine percent of MacNeil/Lehrer's US guests represent elite opinion, while only six percent represent public interest, labor or racial/ethnic organizations . . . ninety percent of its US guests were white and eighty-seven percent were male.[26]

A still later analysis, "Who Spoke on the Gulf?", examined the crisis that culminated in the Persian Gulf War. In the first month of the crisis, when the issues were being defined for the American public, and a genuine debate might have allowed a reasoned policy to be formulated. There was no such debate, on either *Nightline* or the *MacNeil/Lehrer NewsHour*, two of the nation's major public opinion-shaping programs.

> Not a single U.S. guest on *Nightline*, for example, argued against U.S. military intervention. . . . the "experts" used by these shows generally came from conservative think tanks like the American Enterprise Institute and the Center for Strategic and International Studies, with analysts from the centrist Brookings Institution providing the "left" boundary of debate . . . . Less than two percent of *Nightline*'s and less than one percent of *McNeil/Lehrer*'s taped segment subjects represented citizen action groups.

Later, after what should have been the crucial debate period passed, a few critical voices did get heard on the *MacNeil/Lehrer* hour.[27]

The institutionalized absence of critical voices on TV news and public affairs programming is made more palpable still by the heavy representation of conservative and right-wing commentators and shows. In addition to such standbys as the *McLaughlin Group*, William Buckley's *Firing Line*, Evans and Novak, George Will, Fred Barnes, David Gergen (before he joined the Clinton Administration), Patrick Buchanan, and many others of similar persuasion, there is an actual campaign to veil the extent of the narrowness of the prevailing selection process. This is the wilful mislabeling of some of those who are given public access via TV or print. In this charade, mainstream and often moderately conservative individuals are identified as the "left" or at least as countervailing voices to the unabashed rightists. When this is the practice, as it regularly is, the audience is deceived into believing it is watching, and hearing, a genuine clash of views, while nothing of the sort is occurring.

Still, the total media and entertainment enterprise in America is a massive affair. There are hundreds of television stations, thousands of newspapers and magazines, thousands of radio stations, several film studios, and innumerable other outlets of expression. Given the far from homogeneous outlook of the general population, it is to be expected that among the hundreds of thousands of media workers, carefully sifted and instructed as they have been, there still exists a variety of views, some of which may be radical. This is no endorsement of D'Souza and the widespread conservative belief that the radicals are everywhere, and exercise great influence in the presentation of news to the American public. To the contrary, it suggests that the corporate control apparatus, far from being porous or subverted, is able, relatively easily, to neutralize the scattered dissidents.

Indicative of this was the brief flurry over a revelation in late 1988 that *one* reporter working for the *Wall Street Journal*, and then for the *Los Angeles Times*, had been an avowed socialist. A. Kent MacDougall came out of the (socialist) closet with a two-part report in the *Monthly Review*, in which he described his "twenty-four years and nine months in the service of one of the country's major socializing forces—the bourgeois press."[28] The most telling point about MacDougall's "double life" is that it was necessary. If there was such a network of leftist influence in the major media, why would one who shared that viewpoint have to remain underground for a quarter of a century?

But of course the leftist influence doesn't exist. It is the corporate voice that is speaking through the news and public affairs programs. It is hardly noted, much less questioned, that the "objective" *Mc/Neil/Lehrer News-Hour* has had as sponsors New York Life, Pepsico, Archer-Daniels-Midland Co., and other corporate giants. It is these interests that, sometimes directly, but more often in ways that are opaque to the public, insist that the news analysis that Americans receive suits corporate goals.

It is not that Henry Kissinger is so photogenic, or that his voice is so mellifluous that he has been one of the most frequently seen and heard personalities on television for decades, offering his wisdom on current affairs. Initially plucked from the junior faculty at Harvard by the Rockefeller family—his initial appeal to big money resided in his willingness to consider dropping the atom bomb—he has given long and active service to his benefactors. And if the moneyed power selects those who tell us what to think and, equally important, what to think *about*, it also sets the rules for what the dominant news apparatus in the United States deems important to report.

An authority for this assertion is Leslie Gelb, a longtime confidant of the power structure and a former official in the State Department. He was also an editor and senior columnist for the *New York Times*, and most recently,

President of the Council on Foreign Relations. Mr. Gelb told a United Nations' Non-Governmental Organizations' conference in 1991 that "the principal business of journalism consists of recording what people with power say." He also said, "The power of the media resides in its power to choose which ideas to present."[29] This assessment describes precisely and succinctly the current informational situation in the country. The views and opinions of the powerless get short shrift, if any. Yet those without influence suffer no lack of access to the outlooks of the governors. Their views saturate the informational environment.

An almost poignant news dispatch, revealing the impoverishment of the current informational condition in the United States, was the report on graduation speakers at college campuses around the country in June, 1994. It began: "From Connie Chung and Ted Koppel to Cokie Roberts and Andy Rooney, television personalities—most from the network news divisions—are the speakers of choice at many college commencements this year." Others listed included Brit Hume of ABC News and Robert McNeil of the *McNeil/Lehrer NewsHour*.[30] What wisdom could this latest batch of graduates have received in their final college lecture from these highly-paid conduits of processed information? Many of these same individuals, Ken Auletta found, are receiving fat lecture fees from well-heeled organizations and corporations, only too happy to have such influential media voices in their tow. In his *New Yorker* article aptly titled "Fee Speech," some of the other elite commentators mentioned included Sam Donaldson, Cokie Roberts, Brit Hume, David Brinkley, and Robert Novak.[31]

Radio

The mostly invisible filters that sift out critical views in the print and TV media no longer apply to radio broadcasting. Here, a dramatic takeover of the airwaves has replaced relatively subtle message control with hardline ideological bombast. Hundreds of right-wing radio hosts offer highly personalized reactionary doctrine, twenty-four hours a day, seven days a week. Most notable but no longer unique, Rush Limbaugh regales a claimed twenty million listeners via six hundred radio stations that carry his message.[32]

Changing a station's programming to right-wing talk shows is no minor decision. It requires the approval of the station owners. In short, the swamping of the airwaves with right-wing views is a management/investor decision. This is in keeping, as we shall see in the next chapter, with the underlying weakening of democratic institutions.

Overview of the Review and Selection Process in Film, Recording, and Museums

The American film industry brings together, in an unwieldly ensemble, Wall Street money, a half a dozen major film studios (two of which are owned by Japanese transnational corporations), a handful of powerful agents, a cluster of "stars," some established producers, directors, and writers, and a huge periphery of aspiring performers, creative talent, and ancillary service workers. Lastly, and taken into account only as a "market," is the American public.

Making a commercial film, Hollywood observers are fond of saying, is a mixture of art and commerce. Comparing film with dry martini making, the art ingredient is the dash of vermouth. It is there, but it is mostly a trace element. Besides the invariable personal scheming involved in projects that bring together large numbers of people in which the stakes are huge, the ultimate regulator in the thousands of selection decisions required for making a film is the calculation of profitability.

David Putnam, a British film producer and former chairman of Columbia Pictures, in response to a question by Bill Moyers about what kind of men were running Hollywood, noted discreetly: ". . . the job's a very tough job . . . I think that because of the demands of the job, I'm afraid short-term results which are required of all American executives—this is not just the motion picture industry—they are frequently required to make decisions I would argue with . . ."[33] "Short term results," in this context, means the demand for immediate returns, the revered and all-consuming bottom line.

Movies today are expensive undertakings. Will the necessary capital be forthcoming? A run-of-the mill film that offers only modest expectations of box office revenues still may cost ten to twenty million dollars. More ambitious productions, based on published best-sellers or dramatic vehicles, may come in at fifty to eighty million dollars. Promotional budgets for these high-cost products may amount to as much as the original production outlays. In short, Hollywood "blockbuster" films may require an initial expenditure of $100 million or more. In these circumstances, the selection process for script, director, actors, and promoters is market-driven from start to finish; quality is barely considered. What does count is the bankability of the actors and director who can be secured for the film, as well as the suitability of the script to those putting up the money.

This last consideration is the decisive factor in whether the film is made. It is the ultimate step in the filmmaking selection process. It is also the most difficult to trace. The actual reasons for and the locus of decision-making in the acceptance or rejection of the project are obscured by a highly developed public relations branch of the industry, a gossip network that spreads obfuscation, and outright stonewalling from the industry itself. Complicating things further is the large number of individuals who possess veto power, in one way or another, over the undertaking. Those in a position to give a green light are few.

All the same, there is a historical record that offers testimony, retrospectively to be sure, of what has *not* been selected over time as suitable movie themes. The labor movement, workers' rights and struggles, racism, a critical look at anticommunism in post–World War II America, the women's movement, and the labyrinth in mechanics of the military-industrial-scientific power complex are some of the broad areas that have escaped attention, to say nothing of comprehensive coverage. Individual films concerned with one or another of these themes have been produced, but they are the very infrequent exceptions.

In the relatively few films that do take up these subjects, the interpretation or account often contradicts, and seriously confuses or distorts the central theme. One example: In the film *Mississippi Burning*, the positive role the movie assigned to the FBI in the Civil Rights Movement is a gross distortion of reality. The FBI, for decades under J. Edgar Hoover's direction, was one of the greatest obstacles to civil rights, workers' rights, and political freedom of expression.

This is not overreacting to one aberrant film script. Similar distortions characterize most commercial films when they approach subjects that deal with fundamental institutional relationships in America. Hollywood outdoes Washington when it comes to prettifying or eliminating inconvenient terms or basic social divisions. Recent national administrations have fairly effectively written the working class out of the nation's vocabulary. The movies have long been well ahead in this endeavor. *Working Girl* spends little time working, but she's climbing the income ladder at a torrid tempo.

The Writers Guild of America, more than twenty years ago, presented hair-raising testimony by their members on how scripts, or script ideas, were changed or abandoned by network directors or film studios. Though these were accounts of what happened to proposed television shows, the writers' experiences were essentially the same as those working in film, often, the identical individuals. "Writers by the dozen," the Guild representatives stated, "report that they have written characters who are black and have seen them changed to white; they have written Jews and seen them converted to Gentiles; they have proposed shows about South African apartheid, Vietnam, old folks, mental disease, politics, business, labor, students, and minorities; and they have been chased out of studios."[34] One account after another in the testimony detailed the scrubbing of substantive meaning from the proposed materials.

Selection criteria that treat the status quo respectfully are applied with special vigor when the work at hand is provided by independent-minded talent less likely to have succumbed to the lifelong conditioning that is the customary experience of most professionals and white-collar employees. Generally, these filters are sufficient to keep the public insulated from socially provocative material. If the issue is sufficiently compelling and useful to exploit commercially, distorted or sanitized versions are a second line of defense of the status quo. Yet sometimes this protective barrier also gets called into account from an unexpected maverick source. Then, more direct coercive power has to be applied to the source of disturbance.

When a reviewer in *Variety*, the trade journal of show business, for example, had the effrontery to review Paramount Pictures' *Patriot Games*, the $40 million Harrison Ford thriller and denounce it as "fascistic," Paramount, the *Los Angeles Times* reported, was outraged and pulled its advertising. Moreover, the reviewer, a twenty-year veteran of the paper, was given children's movies to review and later dismissed. The editor-in-chief of *Variety* sent an apology to Martin Davis, the chairman and chief executive of Paramount Communications, saying that [the reviewer] was "unprofessional . . . [and] will not review any more Paramount films."[35] The history of journalism is filled with such accounts, most of which scarcely receive mention in the press. They serve as constant reminders to those reporters who may have forgotten what they learned in journalism school and in the newsroom: the interests of the patron, the sponsor, the publisher—in a word, of capital—come first.

Similar lessons are administered, time and again, by the public broadcasting service, which pays far more attention to privileged interests than to the public, who it is supposed to serve. From an unfortunately large sample, one example must suffice. In August 1993, after three years of protests and campaigns, PBS finally aired the documentary *Building Bombs*. The show is an inquiry into what happened at the Savannah River Plant in South Carolina, where hydrogen bombs were made for forty years.

Stalled for three years, the film, when finally screened, was shortened by ten minutes, and forced to leave out entirely one of its two themes: an exploration of the reasons for the Cold War and the nuclear buildup. When originally rejected by PBS in 1990, the producer was told that the basis for rejection was that the documentary "[did] not give adequate voice to those who are proponents of nuclear arms."[36] By claiming that the voice that had prevailed for forty years had been "overlooked," PBS acted to shore up the nuclear power status quo, while at the same time professing even-handedness and balance. The "balance" rationale, a staple of media practice, invariably focuses on one episode and leaves out the historical and social context of the subject being reported. It is almost a guaranteed procedure for achieving a seeming objectivity in the short term, while leaving untouched the full dimensions of the issue.

Lamentably, Public Broadcasting for the most part has succumbed to commercialism and the imperatives that sponsorship demands. Along with the commercials, there is the pathetic effort to placate the Right and carefully comb out programs that might arouse conservative ire. Not unexpectedly, this still does not satisfy the rampaging Right. It clamors to have federal funding for public broadcasting eliminated. At this point, there is precious little to defend in the already-gutted system against the against the attacks of the cultural vandals.

Recording and Museum "Industries"

A few words on the recording industry, an important branch of the cultural industries, are in order. Producing recordings, now largely compact discs and tapes, is big business. It, too, is a concentrated field of activity, owned and controlled by a handful of multinational companies engaged in other cultural production as well. Though corporate rules apply to the recording business no less than to the other media, a couple of characteristics of the industry give it distinctive character.

To begin with, the creative stage of the industry is far less capital intensive and requires much less money to get started than film, TV, or print. A group of musicians with instruments constitutes the initial costs. This relative ease of entry confers more openness on the general character of the industry. Though it should not be exaggerated, it is still true that access is greater in music than it is elsewhere. This makes it possible for more voices, styles, and viewpoints to be expressed in recording than, for example, on television. And they are! Yet how widely their work is distributed is determined largely by the business side of the industry.

The commercial features of recording are no less formidable, and no less ultimately selective, than those in the other cultural spheres. Potentially compelling new groups are acquired by the big labels. Only the large companies can mount the promotional campaigns that launch the group and propel it to national attention. Whatever initial freewheeling quality the group may have had, once in the company fold, an inevitable process of commercialization develops.

The fate of any group depends on its access to radio and TV exposure. This is especially the case for new and not yet well-established groups, and the source of the recurrent "payola" scandals that erupt every few years, after the preceding one has been forgotten. Payola arises from the frenzied promotional efforts of the recording companies to secure air time for their products. "In an average year," one report noted, "more than 5,000 sound recordings are released in the United States, a volume that forces record companies large and small to maintain promotion staffs to make sure the recordings get the broadcast exposure essential to sales." Part of the selection process in the recording industry is as gross as can be imagined. In addition to the initial corporate choices of acquiring this or that group, selection is further abbetted by cruder means. "Radio station program directors say," according to the same report, "that offers of money, drugs, sex, and automobiles in return for broadcasting records are still as common as they have ever been."[37] MTV images apparently mirror the practices in recording offices and studios.

Comparable control factors are no less at work in "high" culture. Writing about museum exhibitions in an age of corporate sponsorship, and general oversight of the cultural selection process, Brian Wallis found a central tendency:

> For a corporation to structure and promote a coherent value system requires a certain control of information and a deliberate constitution of representations. Thus, the selection of exhibitions, as well as presentation of them through advertising, press releases, and even banners, is purposeful and highly calculated. The result is that this self-conscious system of representations—at least as formulated in sponsored exhibitions—tends toward cautionary exclusion, the fixing of stereotypic interpretations, and the development of abstract rather than historically specific concepts. Beyond the obvious "special interests" of corporations . . . most corporate sponsors finance exhibitions based on centrist ideals and uncontroversial subject matter. Hence the proliferation of tame exhibitions . . .[38]

This is a fitting, though only partial, description of the way the review and selection process functions across the cultural-media spectrum in the United States today. In the mid-1990s, a more direct force—unapologetic intervention—is being asserted. For example, an exhibit commemorating the fiftieth anniversary of the dropping of the atomic bomb on Hiroshima was painstakingly prepared for public viewing. Its venue, The Smithsonian Institution, the foremost museum complex in the United States, felt compelled to dismantle the exhibit after protests from some veterans' organizations and legislators. They claimed the United States was being defamed.[39]

Other developments, further weakening the institutions that serve to give American life its democratic texture, are the subject of the next chapter.

Notes

1. Regis Debray, *Teachers, Writers, Celebrities: The Intellectuals of Modern France* (London: Verso, 1981), p. 17.
2. Edward S. Herman and Noam Chomsky, *Manufacturing Consent* (New York: Pantheon, 1988).

3. "Gore, '69, Has Message for Harvard '94," *New York Times*, June 10, 1994, Sec. A, p. 11.
4. Michele Willens, "Where Getting Into Kindergarten Is a Fierce Audition," *New York Times*, September 9, 1993, sec. C, p. 4.
5. Pierre Bourdieu and Jean-Claude Passeron, *Reproduction in Education, Society and Culture* (Newbury Park, CA: Sage, 1977), English edition, p. 141.
6. William Celis 3d, "Michigan Votes for Revolution in Financing Its Public Schools," *New York Times*, March 17, 1994, p. 1.
7. Editorial: "Segregation's Threat to the Economy," *New York Times*, December 19, 1993.
8. Susan E. Brown, "The Zip-Code Route into UC," *Los Angeles Times*, May 3, 1989. Susan Brown, at the time, was director of higher education for the Mexican-American Legal Defense and Education Fund and a member of the San Francisco Civil Rights Commission.
9. Steven Brint and Jerome Karabel, *The Diverted Dream* (New York: Oxford University Press, 1989).
10. Gregory Mantsios, *New York Times Book Review*, December 24, 1989, p. 17.
11. David Karen, review of *The High-Status Track*, edited by Paul William Kingston and Lionel S. Lewis (Albany: State University of New York Press, 1990), in *Science*, Vol. 250, December 21, 1990, pp. 1754–1755.
12. Ben H. Bagdikian, *The Media Monopoly*, Fourth Revised Edition (Beacon Press, 1992), p. ix.
13. Paul DiMaggio and Michael Useem, "The Arts in Class Reproduction," in Michael W. Apple, editor, *Cultural and Economic Reproduction in Education*, (London: Routledge and Kegan Paul, 1982), p. 195.
14. Paul Richter, "Chain Power," *Los Angeles Times*, February 24, 1989. Also, Jon Bekken, ("Concentration in the Retail Book Industry: The Emerging Distribution Monopoly," Mimeo, undated).
15. Steven Weinberg, "The Unruly World of Book Reviews," *Columbia Journalism Review*, March/April, 1990, pp. 51–54.
16. Charles Murphy and Richard Herrnstein, *The Bell Curve* (New York: Basic Books, 1994).
17. Jon Wiener, "Murdered Ink," *Nation*, Vol. 256, Number 21 (May 31, 1993), pp.743–750.
18. Michael Harris, "Wading Into the Watery Grave of Left-Wing Politics," *Los Angeles Times*, April 18, 1994, sec. E, p. 3.
19. Warren Breed, "Social Control in the News Room," *Social Forces*, May, 1955.
20. Bagdikian, *op. cit.*, p. 18.
21. John H. McManus, *Market-Driven Journalism* (Thousand Oaks, CA. Sage, 1994), p.197.
22. Gannett Center *Journal*, Vol. 2, No. 2 (Spring 1988).
23. Ibid.
24. Dinesh D'Souza, "Mr. Donaldson Goes To Washington," *Policy Review*, Vol. 37 (Summer 1986), pp. 24–31.
25. William Hoynes and David Croteau, "Are You On the *Nightline* Guest List?" Fairness and Accuracy in Reporting, February, 1989, pp. 8, 12.

26. William Hoynes and David Croteau, "All the Usual Suspects: *McNeil/Lehrer* and *Nightline*," *Extra*, Vol. 3, No. 4 (Winter, 1990).
27. "Who Spoke on the Gulf?" *Extra*, November/December 1990, p.4.
28. A. Kent MacDougall, "Boring from Within the Bourgeois Press: Parts 1 & 2, *Monthly Review*, November, 1988, pp. 13–24; December, 1988, pp. 10–24.
29. "Peace, Justice and Development Ingredients for an Emerging World," Final Report, Annual Conference of the Department of Public Information for Non-Governmental Organizations, United Nations, New York, September 11–13, 1991, p. 34.
30. William H.. Honan, "For Graduation Speakers, Colleges Are Turning to the Stars of TV News," *New York Times*, May 21, 1994, p. 6.
31. Ken Auletta, "Fee Speech," *New Yorker*, September 12, 1994, pp. 40–47.
32. Timothy Egan, "Triumph Leaves No Targets for Conservative Talk Shows," *New York Times*, January 1, 1995, p. 1.
33. Bill Moyers' "World of Ideas," interview with David Putnam, Part 2, September 16, 1988, Public Affairs Television, WNET/New York.
34. Statement on Behalf of the Writers Guild of America by David Rintels, Norman Lear, and Liam O'Brien. A Senate Committee Judiciary Subcommittee on Constitutional Rights of the Press," February 8, 1972, pp. 515-547.
35. Robert W. Welkos, "A Look Beyond *Variety*'s Story About *Games*," *Los Angeles Times*, August 4, 1992, sec. F, p. 1.
36. Judith Michaelson, "PBS Finally to Air *Building Bombs*, " *Los Angeles Times*, August 10, 1993, sec. F, p. 12.
37. Larry Rohter, "Payola Trial Opens for a Top Record Promoter of the 80's," *New York Times*, August 21, 1990, sec. B, p. 1.
38. Brian Wallis, "Institutions Trust Institutions," in *Hans Haacke: Unfinished Business*, ed. Brian Wallis (Cambridge: M.I.T. Press, 1986), p. 54.
39. Neil A. Lewis, "Smithsonian Substantially Alters Enola Gay Exhibit After Criticism," *New York Times*, October 1, 1994, p. 10.

2

FOR SALE: SCHOOLS, LIBRARIES, INFORMATION, ELECTIONS

For Sale: Public Schools, Public Universities, Public Libraries, Public Information, and Public Elections

As I write this book, an onslaught is underway, mounted with ferocious intensity, against the social philosophy and the legacy of the New Deal. The first Republican-dominated Congress in forty years is enthusiastically engaged in a demolition operation of the social and economic measures, some in place for more than sixty years, protecting the general public against the conditions that existed prior to the Great Depression (those that helped to produce that crisis).

The havoc is still be to realized. Denial of family welfare, children's lunches, and revocation of consumer and worker protective legislation cannot fail, sooner rather than later, to make American life uglier. Yet it would be inaccurate to claim that these actions, or at least the philosophy underlying them, only began with the advent of the 104th Congress in January, 1995. Antecedents in practice and outlook can be traced across the preceding quarter of a century. They accompanied the wrenching shift from general economic buoyancy to protracted crisis that has descended on the United States economy since the early 1970s.

Throughout a good part of American history a continuously rising material standard of living for many, unequal as it was, diverted attention from the profound gaps in the distribution of benefits. The national focus was on general improvement. At the same time, the steady overall economic growth required large numbers of individuals to fill jobs that couldn't be manned exclusively by those from the privileged upper ranks. Accordingly, for a long time there was substantial upward social movement for considerable numbers of individuals and families. A large fraction—though still a minority—of the population moved into and enjoyed the comfort and status of middle-class life.

The post–World War II years, until the mid-1970s, reinforced and broadened this condition. The economic benefits of being the strongest industrial and military state were appropriated mostly by the super corporations and the already well off. But, all the same, there was a trickle down of material advantage to the working population as well. Not least in this benefit stream were the relatively full employment, the good pay, the better (suburban) housing, and the great expansion of the educational system, especially at the college and university levels.

None of these developments uprooted or overturned the structural elements in American life that produce inequality and differential opportunity. Yet they succeeded well enough in largely muting whatever dissatisfaction there may have been. They served also to encourage the belief that the profound, crisis-provoking elements, so evident in the 1930s, had either been eliminated or bypassed. For a relatively brief period, there flourished what John Kenneth Galbraith has described as a "Culture of Contentment."[1]

Contentment, although at no time in the past evenly experienced across all income groups, hardly expresses current popular sentiment. The end of the Cold War and the return of economic crisis—no random relationship—has brought back the reality of American social structure. As the pressure on the economy from foreign competition intensifies and the formerly Cold War–inspired government military expenditures diminish, increasing numbers of Americans are facing conditions that have not existed since the 1930s. How fares the general well-being of the people in a time of contraction? More long-lastingly, how fare the democratic institutions that provided Americans with some space to press for improvement of the less-advantaged majority?

Historically, the review and selection process did the job of weeding and sifting, and guaranteeing the placement of the advantaged in the command slots of the social order. Yet throughout the long-term period of its application, the idea of and the institutions associated with the common good and the public interest remained intact—on occasion, strengthened. The belief continued to exist that there was something beyond individual advantage, and that community came before self. There were also practical institutions that defended this view. These constituted the bedrock of the national democratic heritage and its living practice.

Widespread, continuous, and serious departures from these principles and practices, in the past, by the nation's rich and powerful interests, repeatedly inflicted great damage on the democratic order. Yet the structures of democratic governance—public schools, public libraries, the electoral system of representation, local governments, nonprofit organizations—buffetted and handicapped as they often have been, survived, and generated democratic impulses with surprising frequency. No longer can this be said unqualifiedly!

Beginning in the 1980s and accelerating in the 1990s, the centers of democratic life and activity are either being dismantled and abandoned, or their functions transformed and their missions reversed. The changes, occurring at varying speeds across the entire economy, and especially its educational-cultural sphere, are profoundly altering the basic nature of American society. And, true to good public relations practice, these developments are presented—even hailed—as improvements and enhancements of democratic life. Newt Gingrich, for example, in his first remarks after assuming his new job as Speaker of the House of Representatives, lauded the vision and placed Franklin D. Roosevelt as a great leader of the twentieth century. Almost in the same breath, he launched his Republican forces on a course to undo and eliminate as much as possible of what remained of FDR's New Deal.

The destruction of the *belief* in the common good, and the rejection of the costs required for achieving it, are especially evident in what is happening to the nation's schools. The idea of *schools being public* has come into question. Efforts are multiplying either to withdraw schools from public authority, or to transform their character from within by far-reaching structural changes. No one denies that the nation's public schools, especially but not exclusively in the poorer districts and urban neighborhoods, are atrocious. *But why are these deplorable conditions reason to abandon, or drastically undercut, the principle of public education?* Is it because democratic—free, openly available, community accountable, and adequately supported—schools are no longer of importance to a social order that does not know what to do with an existing schooled population? Or is profit-making, not content with its presence in most of national life, now seeking new sources of revenues and new terrain in which to operate? It is both.

Schools as Profit Centers

There are many things terribly out of joint in America's public school system. Most briefly, there are underpaid and, consequently, undereducated teachers. Some schools are decrepit and malfunctoning as structures. There are enormous problems arising from educating youngsters of widely varying background and preparation. Many of these are the children of the heavy migrations to the United States in the Cold War years, coming from countries that were pawns in the U.S.-Soviet struggle. Many others are African American youths, whose parents or grandparents were uprooted from the agricultural South during and after World War II. These families come from backgrounds of three hundred years or more of economic and cultural deprivation. There are the children from Mexico and Central America, refugees from countries either in the grip of coercive U.S.-supported regimes or from countries that tried to make changes in their social structure and suffered U.S. military interventions, directly or by proxy. And there are the children from the white working class with their parents' hopes and prospects in tatters, and the children from the one-parent families, where, for most, there is an epic daily struggle merely to survive.

For good or ill, these are today's children. Only a national mobilization of resources, comparable to those undertaken to wage the two World Wars in this century, could begin to meet their manifold needs. Instead, there have been savage cutbacks of educational budgets and other social programs, locally and nationally, to manage the fiscal disarray that four decades of militarization, financial speculation, and the anticommunism crusade have produced.

It is into this near-chaotic educational scene, and its desperate resource needs, that entrepreneurialism has come, bringing minimal resources but with maximum hopes of *extracting profits*. Two techniques to achieve this objective have been adopted to date. One is to take over the management of existing public schools on a contractual basis with the local school system; the other is to provide new teaching technologies for which certain payments in kind are made.

In the takeover option, sometimes called "charter schools," the private company or group receives the funds that otherwise would have gone to the public school system. The private managers introduce their presumed cost effective measures and take a cut of the expected savings. The takeover option has been increasingly adopted in several parts of the country: in Baltimore, fifteen schools to date; in Massachusetts, the entire Hartford school system; Florida; California; and elsewhere. In some instances, the private administrators come from nationally-formed companies such as the Edison Project, a former Whittle initiative, and the Minnesota-based Education Alternatives. In others, local groups have been organized to manage the schools.

Whatever its specific organizational form, the privately-managed school diminishes the legitimacy of the public school *concept*, weakens the public school structure, and affects for the worse, other democratic institutions as well. How this works is illustrated by some of the "cost effective" measures these new arrangements introduce. One is to hire college students as teachers' aides at $7 an hour, replacing $13-an-hour union members. Tenure to teachers, union work rules, and pay scales are out. Nonunion school custodians are hired to replace union members.[2] Following American industry's practices over the last two decades, the school privatizers mainly target organized labor for cost-cutting and elimination.

Voluntarism also ranks high in the plans of the privatizers. Parents, and the school children themselves, will be called upon to clean and maintain the buildings and classrooms. Most of the schools that have entered into these arrangements thus far are in areas where the poor and minorities are concentrated, and dependence on voluntarism would seem to be a highly unreliable support. Can already overworked and underpaid families provide additional unpaid labor for their children's schooling?

Another feature given great emphasis in the privately run programs is technology. Hope is expressed as fact that computers and ancillary equipment will facilitate learning and reduce costs. The costs, mentioned softly, if at all, are the salaries of live teachers. The belief in the capabilities of equipment, especially high-tech items, to overcome social problems is a pervasive notion in the country, frequently expressed at the presidential level. Application of high tech to youngsters' education may be, *at best*, of limited supplemental value. Its capacity to provide the full educational menu is a delusion, if not a willful deception. (See chapters 5 and 6 for an extended discussion of the role of technology as a means of overcoming social problems.)

It is still too early to judge the educational effects of turning public schools over to private, for-profit interests. In any case, results will be difficult to measure because the overall impact affects far more than individual test scores and achievement tests. One locale's "success," or "failure" is almost irrelevant to the main thrust of the current efforts. What matters is that an entire system and its approach to education and public accountability are being swept aside. The effects of breaking up the public school system radiate throughout the social order.

As far-reaching as the changing of school management from public to private is, it has been preceded by an at least an equally powerful transformation in the public school curriculum in more than 12,000 secondary schools to date. Here is the way it is described by a major executive of the original company that initiated the program:

> The Whittle Educational Network (WEN) has a serious commitment to providing quality programming and technology to America's secondary schools. WEN was developed in 1989 in response to the concern of parents and teachers in local communities who were seeking innovative public/private partnerships to provide resources for under-supported schools. With an investment of more than $300 million, WEN represents the largest single infusion of video technology and programming to secondary schools in United States history.[3]

Who would be churlish enough to dispute such noble intentions and objectives? All the comforting words and terms are assembled in *one* paragraph: "serious commitment," "quality programming," "concerns of parents and teachers," "local communities," "innovative public/private partnerships," "resources for under-supported schools," and so on.

What is the full reality of the former Whittle, now K-III Company, Channel 1 program, broadcast to over 12,000 secondary schools and viewed by eight million teenagers across the country? How well does it meet the deep teacher and parental concerns over education, a woefully undersupported school system, the lack of quality programming, and the need for local initiatives?

Many schools are financially pressed and cannot afford the satellite receiver dishes, the television monitors, and the videocassette recorders that the former Whittle Corporation makes available to the schools that join up in the "public/private partnership." Initially, the partnership brought together the Whittle Corporation, 37% owned by super conglomerate Time Warner (and 13% by Philipps, a Dutch electronics giant) and an impoverished high school. Some partnership! The constituents of this partnership have changed. In the summer of 1994 the Whittle Corporation, literally insolvent, sold its Channel 1 network to K-III Communication Corp., a subsidiary of a still larger financial conglomerate.[4]

What does K-III Communication extract for its free provision of electronic gear to the participating schools? Along with this "gift," K-lll produces and transmits—and the schools must accept—ten minutes of televised currrent events, "news," which is also free. The one condition is that the kids must watch an additional two minutes of commercials that the company tags onto the current events. It is from these televised advertisements for candy, clothes, accessories, running shoes, etc., that K-III Communication earns its income from the sponsors of the advertised products.

Focusing on the well-known educational deficiencies of millions of school children, K-III claimed at the outset that it was providing a means to overcome these shocking inadequacies. Leaving aside the "news" material, which at best is a jazzed-up dilution of the already thin fare adults receive, the school space has become a major marketing venue. The company's spokespeople say the kids see commercials at home all the time, so what difference does it make that they see a few more for an extra couple of minutes a day? *Does* it make a difference?

The child and the teenager do encounter in their daily routines at home, on television, in the movies, at sports events, the same messages and images that celebrate and promote consumption. In these communications democracy comes to be defined as the act of choosing . . . goods. More and more public schools, with the help of the K-III Educational Network, have become marketing-saturated image and message environments. Public space, free of corporate imagery, is an increasingly rare feature of the American social and physical landscape.[5]

The most recent literal expression of this near-total envelopment of public education by commerce is the so-called "mall school." In the biggest shopping mall in America, in Bloomington, Minnesota, a public high school puts the kids in classrooms abutting Sears, Macy's, Bloomingdale's, Burger King, Sunglass Hut International, etc. The rationale: that's where the kids like to hang out and that's where their parents go. Also, it can provide on-site "internships" in retailing to the mostly working-class youngsters who attend the school. These "innovative" arrangements, sprouting in malls across the country, supplemented with Channel 1 TV broadcasts, enable commerce to surround and occupy public school space and children's minds. Or, more benignly put: "All Under One Roof: Shopping and Education."[6]

With imagination, the commercialization of school space can be carried further still. One enterprising school district "has begun selling advertising space in its gymnasiums, in its hallways, in its school buses, and in its newsletters . . . Pupils at one elementary school travel in bright yellow buses painted with the round red spots that sell 7-Up. Burger King ads, designed with the help of students, are painted on other district buses."[7]

The privatization and commercialization of United States' public education proceeds swiftly, pushed forward relentlessly by the country's economic crisis and, equally, by the unwillingness of the political leadership to undertake the massive redistribution of resources and income that might alleviate the accompanying social crisis. Indeed, the Congressional political leadership in place in 1995 considers its highest duty the protection and well being of private property. Redistribution of income and resources in the current environment doesn't stand a chance.

Privatization is not experienced only at the elementary and high school levels. A two-pronged movement is accomplishing the same result in higher education. As state budgets grow more pinched, their allocations for state-supported college and universities are reduced. An editorial in *Science* noted:

> Public support of higher education as a percentage of its overall cost is constantly diminishing . . . California, once the leader in state-supported, tuition-free higher education [now gets] 37% of its operating budget from the state and must make up the rest from tuition fees and alumni support.[8]

The schools' funding alternatives are limited. They can raise tuition—which they do. They can reduce operations by cutting back on classes and faculty—which they do. And they can seek corporate support for particular fields of learning which are of interest to business, e.g., molecular biology, electrical engineering, computer science—which they increasingly do. Each of these alternatives contributes to the erosion of public higher education. In the first two instances, entry into and continuation in universities and colleges becomes more difficult for students. As tuition rises, increasing numbers of applicants are priced out of the system. As classes and teachers are cut back, it is difficult for students to get the courses they need for graduation. The period of attendance is extended, the costs are increased, and those with less ability to pay drop out of the system.

In the spring of 1994 a new "breakthrough" in American higher education was publicized. The leading private colleges in the nation announced their tuition schedules for 1994–5. The costs for a four-year degree exceeded $100,000 for the first time. Admittedly, this affected relatively small numbers of students attending the elite schools: Harvard, Yale, M.I.T., Brown, Stanford, and a few others. Yet similar increases, if less astronomical in their total, were also set for state universities and colleges.

"The responsibility for paying for higher education," notes one observer, "is being shifted from taxpayers [actually, the community] to students and their families." The effect of this is that "We're heading troward a price-based admission policy where the people who can afford it will go to college and the others won't." What this trend, underway for several years, already has done to the democratic ideal of equal opportunity is striking. "In 1979, a student whose family income was in the top quartile [25%] had a four times greater chance of earning a B.A. degree by the age of twenty-four than did a student in the lowest quartile. Today, that well-off student has a nineteen times better chance."[9] Given these ratios, the review and selection process in the time ahead may be easier to pursue because the numbers of qualified candidates for jobs may be fewer. The stability of the social order, however, may be another story.

Finally, the increasing corporate presence on the nation's campuses, especially at more well-endowed universities, deserves a book of its own. Here, it can only be said that as university-business ties thicken, the allocation of resources and faculty are tilted to the money-making part of the curriculum. Less attention is paid to the nonprofit university sectors: humanities, some of the social sciences, and so on. The purposes of a higher education become increasingly blurred, where they are not already openly identified with corporate goals. (For a comprehensive discussion of these developments, Lawrence Soley's *Leasing the Ivory Tower* is a good primer.[10])

Information: Commodity or Social?

Less visible, but no less damaging to the common good, is the character of the large-scale transformation in recent decades of information. World War II, and the Cold War that followed it, were the stimuli for vast governmental expenditures on research, development, and new information technologies. The huge amounts of data produced required new modes for its organization, classification, storage, and distribution. This was provided by the computers developed to handle military logistics and to manage the worldwide mobilization of men, resources, and equipment in the war and postwar periods. The mountains of data and the growing stock of information processing equipment are the essential elements in the information-using economy, the alleged "information society" that has emerged in recent years.

But information and data-processing instrumentation are not independent or autonomous elements in society. How, and for what purposes, they are employed constitute essential and defining features of the social order. In the case of information, two dramatically different ways of using it can be imagined. One is to regard information as a social good and a central element in the development and creation of a democratic society. Under this premise, information serves to facilitate democratic decision making, assists citizen participation in government, and contributes to the search for roughly egalitarian measures in the economy at large. Comprehensive and well-organized information enables decision makers to make rational resource allocation decisions; to prioritize social claims; to maximize social welfare. It allows them to overcome baleful practices that harm the general welfare, like pollution, smoking, and armaments production. Such information resources allow leaders to promote the development of science and invention that are socially beneficial and to organize historical experience for meaningful contemporary reflection and use. In brief, comprehensive, well-organized public information enables decision makers to bring past knowledge and experience to bear on current issues and problems.

In contrast to information as a social good, a different approach can treat information as a privately produced commodity for sale. Actually, since Gutenberg, information has been bought and sold. Yet in the 500-year evolution of the industrial-capitalist state, social movements have sought to reserve some share of the community's information production and supply for common use. The public library system and the great land-grant universities are among the signal achievements of these efforts in the United States.

In the 1990s, with the indispensable assistance of computerization, information is being produced, packaged, stored, and sold. Public stockpiles of information, governmental and academic, are being acquired in all sorts of imaginative and pecuniary ways by private companies. A vigorous and aggressive private Information Industry Association successfully promotes its own objectives. In this pervasive atmosphere of privately acquiring, processing, and selling information, the public library system, a long-standing custodian of the idea and practice, of information as a social good, is tottering. Its function is being redefined and stripped of its social character.

The *Chronicle of Higher Education*, in May, 1994, carried this headline in its information technology section: "New Era for Library Schools: They strive to overhaul curricula to reflect the explosion in information technology." The *Chronicle's* reporter gave these details about the general overhaul underway in library schools across the country: schools are looking for ways to teach technology; "Administrators are hiring information-systems specialists, rather than traditional library educators"; "Administrators are recruiting technically oriented students"; new accreditation criteria have been adopted that "will evaluate library curricula under standards that 'reflect technology in their entirety.'" In many instances, "schools have begun adding 'information' and 'science' to their names" and dropping the "library" designation.[11]

Real problems do exist. In the 1980s "growth decade," "twelve accredited [library] schools, or approximately one-fifth of the total, closed. One by one, SUNY at Geneseo, Mississippi, Minnesota, Western Michigan, Ball State, Case Western, Denver, Southern California, Emory, George Peabody College, and Chicago reached the conclusion that library education was not good business." In 1990, Columbia University, whose library school was the first of its kind in the United States, announced its decision to close the school.[12] In 1994 the library school at Berkeley, at the University of California, was down-sized and reorganized.

Is technological backwardness, even librarians' alleged technophobia, the source of American libraries' and library schools' difficulties? Will the abandonment of the word "library," and the conversion of library education from social service ideals to near-exclusive attention to information-processing instrumentation, restore vitality to the field? Is this an accurate diagnosis of the problem?

In truth, American libraries and the profession of librarianship are confronted with a structural transformation in the overall economy. It is nothing less than thorough privatization of the information function. The production, processing, storing and transmitting of information have been scooped up into private, for-profit hands. Social sources and repositories of information have been taken over for commercial use and benefit. It is not because American libraries and library schools have fallen behind in the mastery of the new information technology that their existence increasingly is called into question. It is their bedrock principles and long-term practices that collide with the realities of today's corporate-centered and market-driven economy. The extent to which librarians insist on free and untrammeled access to information, "unrestricted by administrative barriers, geography, ability to pay or format," they will be treated by the privatizers as backward-looking, if not obsolete, irrelevant, and unrealistic.[13]

The technology issue, therefore, is merely a screen behind which a far-reaching and socially regressive institutional change has occurred. The focus on technology also serves to delude many, librarians included, that the new means to achieve status and respect is to concentrate on the *machinery* of information, production, and transmission. When and if this focus turns rigidly exclusive, wittingly or not, the *social* basis of the profession and the needs of the majority of the people are left unattended.

Actually, there is no need for librarians or others to be technophobes or rejectionists of the new information technologies. In the information field, the new technologies have their greatest potential application, *if the social question is put foremost*. There is every reason to be enthusiastic over the possibilities of new communication capabilities. But there is more reason to be concerned with what will be the character of the utilization of these new means and techniques. Accordingly, there is no inherent incompatibility in offering more technologically-oriented courses in a library school and maintaining, indeed, expanding, the school's attention to the social uses of the new instrumentation. This, in fact, should be the aim of a new librarianship curriculum—how to guarantee social use and application of the new information technologies. But this is not what is happening. Instead, there are different vistas.

Illustrative is an article with the upbeat title, "Here Come the 'Infopreneurs.'" It explains: "In the old days, they were known as librarians. Today, information-brokers wend their way through hundreds of computer databases with the greatest of ease."[14] At a fee to be sure. Another straw in the wind: The conference theme for the June 1994 113th Annual Conference of the American Library Association, chosen by the Association's president, was "Customer Service: The Heart of the Library." John Berry, the editor-in-chief of *Library Journal*, had this to say about this choice: "My dictionary defines 'customer' as 'a person who purchases goods or services from another,' so I hope librarians expand the 'service' idea to all who need library service, not just the customers."[15]

Admittedly, these are hardly consequential episodes. Yet they are suggestive of the forces now shaping and changing the role of the public and academic library—and the self-image of librarians as well! It is the burgeoning buying and selling of information, according to the "customer's" ability to pay, that is forcing librarians to yield their historic role as guardians of the public's right to free and unrestricted information. Assuredly, commercial information activities have an important function to fulfill. Yet to imagine that these services are the sum total of a librarian's contribution—as information broker—is to acquiesce in the emergence of a society in which social aims have been discarded.

Many librarians resist this direction and work valiantly, sometimes successfully, in the democratic tradition, defending the general social good. Their efforts are part of a larger democratic struggle that is not going well at this time. Alongside besieged public schools and public libraries are other organizations and institutions with democratic objectives and agendas that are also being swamped by technological, financial, and political pressures of the voracious market economy.

Nonprofit Organizations Pulled into the Commercial Nexus

The United States possesses a rich fabric of voluntary and nonprofit organizations and groups that constitute what is called "civil society." Civil society is a crucial locus of democratic culture where the many voices of the general community express their views, argue their positions, and seek to gain adherents. Independence of expression is an inalienable condition of civil society's health and vitality.

Today, in at least one important sector of civil society, this independence is threatened by an increased corporate presence, often voluntarily sought, that attaches itself to the undertakings of nonprofit organizations. "Increasingly," a *Los Angeles Times* report, pointedly titled, "Public Good or Private Gain?" notes, "groups such as the NOF [National Osteoporis Foundation], Arthritis Foundation, National Safe Kids Campaign, the American Cancer Society, and dozens of others have gratefully accepted corporate funding to help them promote their causes."

These pacts derive from two pervasive conditions in the current economy. One is the more or less general financial inability of most nonprofits to publicize their aims and objectives and to carry on their work effectively. The other is the corporate effort either to gain market share for a drug or product related to the nonprofit's work, or to burnish its image as good citizen. These divergent motivations produce some remarkably curious and questionable link-ups that are being brought to the public's attention via TV and the press. Some examples:

—A *Playboy* ad given free of charge to the National Breast Cancer Coalition. The ad, worth $167,000, features a baby breast-feeding and a smart-alecky caption: addressed to the magazine's mostly male readership, "You've probably been a breast man since day one." Unquestionably, it gets more attention than would an earnest public service appeal.

—A half-hour infomercial, financed by pharmaceutical powerhouse Smith-KlineBeecham in agreement with the National Osteoporosis Foundation, launching a new calcium supplement (Tums 500) that was supposed to help prevent osteoporosis. The Foundation was satisfied that the program got its message across—the causes and dangers of osteoporosis—to a national audience.

—An Arthritis Foundation ad financed by the makers of Tylenol.

Jay Winsten, director of the Center for Health Communications at the Harvard School of Public Health, says that these deals are "win, win, win for everyone." "Health groups get exposure," notes the *Los Angeles Times'* interviewe with the Director, "at the same time as the sponsor gets either to promote a product or polish its image." Less sanguine about these activities is Michael Jacobson, co-founder of the Washington, D.C., Center for the Study of Commercialism. "In hard times," he observes, "it's hard to be too much of a purist. But over the long run, the nonprofit sector is being jeopardized.[16]

The reason most nonprofit organizations were created to begin with was to fill a public need not being met by private enterprise. Accepting corporate help, however threatened the nonprofits' economic viability may be, is to relinquish still another bulwark of the public interest to the already-commanding corporate realm. Can a public, nonprofit organization safely accept an association with a corporate sponsor whose self-interest has little, if anything, to do with the nonprofit organization's goals, to say nothing of the general common good? The answer would seem to be self-evident. Unfortunately for the common good, these slippery associations are proliferating. They are present as well, and growing tighter, in many other public sector spheres, e.g., noncommercial television.

Representative Democracy—An Oxymoron?

Public schools, public libraries, and a vigorous public sector (civil society) are among the essential elements, the underpinning, of a democratic order. That order itself finds its ultimate expression in its system of governance. Representative government, wherein the citizenry elect their representatives to carry on the daily processes of decision making, is the proud and preeminent institution of democracy. Endless volumes have been written about the history, evolution, strengths, and weaknesses of electoral politics. And here are two observations relevant to the overall theme of this book, the present state of the common good, and its information condition in particular.

Today, much of the authority of government in most countries, representative or not, is being usurped by extraterritorial and extranational forces. Some call these developments "globalization." For the most part, the main players in this game are the private superbusinesses operating around the globe. Their activities, how they affect national governance, and what their longterm impact is, also will be considered in later chapters. It is sufficient to note here that representative democracy, wherever it exists, is gravely injured by this global phenomenon.

There is another equally important, but mostly domestically-generated condition, that further limits, and undermines, representative democracy. It is the money power and it has succeeded in massively distorting the election process. In fact, it has served to largely privatize it. American politics and elections today are about money—who has it, who can get it, will it be enough? One reporter put it this way:

> From the outside, running for office looks like a stream of television commercials, sound bites and public forums. But the real business of campaigns is conducted out of public view. And the real business is money . . . This is the underbelly of American politics.[17]

In a country approaching a population of 250 million people, direct access to potential voters—the old barnstorming of earlier years—is totally out of the question. When a candidate actually appears before a group of citizens, it is more for ritual than for practical effect, and, in any case, the candidate hopes the appearance will be televised.

Television, opinion polling, focus groups, and elaborate voter profile construction are the contemporary elements of election campaigning. Each costs money and television costs the most. Reporting about California politics, the most important in the country because of the size and population of the state, one account noted that "few candidates can raise the money needed to reach all of the state with television advertisements, not at the usual cost of $40,000 for a thirty-second spot in prime time."[18]

The price of prime national-TV time is astronomical. It doesn't occur to those who govern the political system that commercial TV companies might be obligated to give the time free of charge. This is not an extraordinary demand. The companies are using a public natural resource, the radio spectrum—for which they pay no fees. The spectrum belongs to the people, as do the national preserves and the oceans and rivers—though part of it is now being sold off to private owners. (See chapter 6.)

Money to buy television time so that the candidate will be known to the public can come from only a few sources: personal wealth, others' wealth, grassroots donations. Dependence on the latter is, with few exceptions, unrealistic. So, either one has money of one's own or one can tap others' funds. In either case, a very special kind of candidate emerges. In the 1990s, elections—locally and especially nationally—offer representation almost exclusively to the moneyed interest. Candidates, so annointed, may still possess personal views that are sympathetic to the public's interest. Yet the golden ties that bind are rarely absent from today's elected officials. To participate seriously in the 1996 national elections, a candidate must raise a $40 million campaign fund. To start out with less than $25 million in hand is regarded as unrealistic. How many "realistic" aspirants can there be in the country and what is the source of their special status?

Overall, the health of American democratic institutions on the threshold of the twenty-first century is precarious. It is all the more so when a close look is taken at the country's informational structure and practices.

Notes

1. John Kenneth Galbraith, *The Culture of Contentment* (Boston: Houghton-Mifflin, 1992).
2. William Celis 3d., "Hartford Seeking a Company to Run Its Public Schools, *New York Times*, April 19, 1994. Also, Peter Passell, "Public Schools for Profit, Phase 2: The Sales Pitch," *New York Times,* January 19, 1994, sec. B, p. 8.

3. Scott Helbing (Executive Vice-president/Senior Partner, Whittle Educational Network, Whittle Communications), *Intermedia,* Vol. 22, No. 1 (1994), p. 4.

4. John Lippman, "Whittle to Sell Channel 1," *Los Angeles Times*, August 10, 1994.

5. Herbert I. Schiller, *Culture Inc.: The Corporate Takeover of Public Expression* (New York: Oxford University Press, 1989).

6. Michael Winerip, "All Under One Roof: Shopping and Education," *New York Times,* May 2, 1994, sec. A, p. 1.

7. "A School District is Selling Ad Space," *New York Times*, November 19, 1994, p. 17.

8. Daniel E. Koshland, Jr., "The Opportunity Connection," *Science,* Vol. 267, February 24, 1995, p. 1075.

9. William H. Honan, "The $100,000 Quest: A College Degree," *International Herald Tribune,* May 6, 1994, p. 3.

10. Lawrence C. Soley, *Leasing the Ivory Tower* (Boston: South End Press, 1995.)

11. Beverly T. Watkins, "New Era for Library Schools," *Chronicle of Higher Education,* May 18, 1994, Vol. 40, No. 37, p. A19.

12. Deanna B. Marcum, "Library Education: A Challenge for the 1990s," *Bowker Annual*, 1991, 36th edition.

13. American Library Association, Government Documents Roundtable (GODORT), February 1991.

14. *Sky,* Delta Airlines, November, 1990, p. 78.

15. John Berry, "Program Picks and Pans," *Library Journal,* Vol. 119, No. 10 (June 1, 1994), p. 54.

16. Shari Roan, "Public Good or Private Gain?" *Los Angeles Times,* May 31, 1994, p. 1.

17. Richard L. Berke, "Before Asking for Votes, Candidates Ask for Cash," *New York Times,* May 10, 1994, p. 1.

18. B. Drummond Ayres, Jr., "California Primary Sets a Lavish Tone, Lifting a Long Shot," *New York Times,* June 7, 1994, p. 1.

3

DATA DEPRIVATION

Data Deprivation

An all-embracing structural transformation of the last fifty years has been the ascendance of corporate power and the corresponding decline of government authority over key areas of national economic, political, and social life. This has occurred in all industrialized as well as less developed economies, though with considerable variability from one country to another.

In the United States, where this change is most fully developed, it is also less evident because of the continuing, though declining, global hegemonic role of the American state. This requires a huge military, intelligence, and police apparatus to monitor and discipline the far-flung territories as well as a potentially disaffected domestic public. This vast apparatus, now being reluctantly downsized, still confers great power on the state. The trend, however, has been to extend private decision making at the expense of governmental authority.

In the increasingly central spheres of communication and information, the shift from state to private power is especially marked and observable. Here, too, exceptional conditions conceal the full dimensions of the transfer of authority. Not least is the capability of the private informational machine to withhold the evidence of its own primacy and activity. Additionally, there is the continuing barrage, issuing from the same source, of an "information glut," and the burdens of living in an "information society." This clamor serves to divert attention from the very real, but largely invisible, deficit of socially necessary information.

What are the effects of the enormous extension of private power in the informational sphere? They can be appreciated best, perhaps, by considering what has been happening to individual expression, and how this is explained. Historically, the threat to individual expression has been seen to come from an arbitrary state. This view is embodied in the U.S. Constitution where free speech is explicitly protected against governmental power and its potential for abuse. And so it has been for centuries; states limiting

43

and suppressing individual expression, and individuals and social movements struggling to reduce and overcome censorial power.

A new condition now exists, though it is one that is barely acknowledged! What distinguishes this era is that the main threat to free expression has shifted from government to private corporate power. This does not imply that the state has lost its taste for controlling individual expression. It means instead that a more pervasive force has emerged that now constitutes a stronger and more active threat to such expression.

Today, the power of huge, private, economic enterprises is extended across national and international boundaries, influencing and directing economic resource decisions, political choices, and the production and dissemination of messages and images. The American economy is now hostage to a relatively small number of giant private companies, with interlocking connections, that set the national agenda. This power is particularly characteristic of the communication and information sector where the national cultural-media agenda is provided by a very small (and declining) number of integrated private combines.[1] This development has deeply eroded free individual expression, a vital element of a democratic society.

At the same time, the new private information power centers strive actively and, to date, successfully to persuade the public that their corporate message- and image-making activity is a daily exercise in individual free expression. This effort relies heavily on a century-old Supreme Court ruling that the corporation is an individual. It follows from this extravagant interpretation that the threat to individual expression can come only from the state.

How this logic works is exemplified in a full-page advertisement in the *New York Times* in which the Freedom Forum Foundation approvingly quotes the view of Supreme Court Justice, Thurgood Marshall: "If the First Amendment means anything, it means that a state has no business telling a man, sitting alone in his own house, what books he may read or what films he may watch. Our whole constitutional heritage rebels at the thought of giving government the power to control men's minds."[2] And so it does! Readers of the ad might not know that the Freedom Forum is the creation of the Gannett Corporation, one of the nation's largest media combines, owner of a country-wide chain of local papers and the national newspaper, *USA Today*. The Gannett enterprise precisely fits the definition of a media conglomerate, heavily dependent on corporate advertising revenues, disseminating carefully processed material to millions of readers and viewers.

In quoting Justice Marshall's cautionary words, the Gannett Corporation is identifying its powerful, nationally expressed voice as individual expression. At the same time it is deflecting attention from its oversized influence on popular opinion and shifting the nation's focus to the older and familiar concern, state control of expression. Where once there was justified fear of government control and censorship of speech, today there is a new form of censorship, structurally pervasive, grounded in private concentrated control of the media, and generally undetectable in a direct and personal sense.

Marshall's words, were they to include the new reality, could well be recast: If the First Amendment means anything, it means that a media combine has no business telling an individual, sitting alone in that person's own house, what books to read or what films to watch. Our whole constitutional heritage rebels at the thought of giving giant information corporations the power to control peoples' minds.

There is more than enough justification for this reformulation of traditional free speech doctrine. What American voices, other than corporate ones, can afford to pay half a million dollars or more for a thirty-second TV commercial on national television? Elder statesman George Kennan recently reflected: "As things stand today, without advertising presumably very little of the communications industry would survive."[3] Given these economic realities, much of the space in the American cultural house has been appropriated for corporate messages. This has become literally so. Atlanta, for example, is seriously considering renaming some of its streets and parks with corporate logos, "Coca-Cola Boulevard" and "Georgia Pacific Park" to raise funds.[4]

Corporate speech has become a dominant discourse, nationally and internationally. It has also dramatically changed the context in which the concepts of freedom of speech, a free press, and democratic expression have to be considered. While the corporate voice booms across the land, individual expression, at best, trickles through tiny constricted public circuits. This has allowed the effective right to free speech to be transferred from individuals to billion dollar companies which, in effect, monopolize public communication.[5]

Corporate influence now penetrates almost every social space. One of its earliest and continuing efforts has been to shake off, or at least greatly reduce, the relatively modest restraints imposed on its economic and social decision making. These limitations derived from the populist and reform movements of the late nineteenth century and the devastating impact of the Great Depression in the 1930s. The rapacious behavior of the industrial monopolies that emerged after the Civil War, and the social misery that accompanied the economic crisis of sixty years ago, compelled the political leadership of those times to produce a variety of protective social measures. These included Social Security, bank and financial regulations, communication and transport rules, and labor's right to organize. The upsurge of the civil rights, feminist, and anti–Vietnam War movements in the 1960s introduced additional social protections. Undeniably, these also interfered with the freedom of corporations to ignore such matters.

Since the end of World War II, and especially the last twenty-five years, corporate power has countered these developments with intensive and largely successful efforts. It has pressed to remove the machinery of socially responsible supervision. This goes under the name of deregulation. It has led the campaign to privatize a variety of activities and functions that had been under public administration. And it has sought to extend market relationships to new spheres of rapidly growing economic activity, e.g., information management.

Deregulation, privatization, and the expansion of market relationships have affected all corners of the economy. Here, only the impact on the national information condition—no peripheral area—will be considered. The generation and provision of information and entertainment, and the technology that makes it possible, are among the most dynamic elements in the economy. How these are put together profoundly affects the character of the national information condition. The hope is always that they will constitute the basis for an informed population and a democratic social order. In fact, when the effects of privatization, deregulation, and expanded market relationships are added to the corporate near-monopoly on public communication channels, a deep, though not generally visible, erosion in the national information infrastructure can be detected.

Bill McKibben, in *The Age of Missing Information,* reflects on the loss of understanding of nature and its ways.

> I've tried to describe some of the information that the modern world—the TV world—is missing. Information about the physical limits of a finite world. About sufficiency and need, about proper scale and real time, about the sensual pleasure of exertion and exposure to the elements, about the human need for community and for solid, real skills.[6]

McKibben is calling attention to a real loss. But here, I am examining another kind of missing information. It is a consequence of a warped social institutional environment.

The spectacularly improved means of producing, organizing, and disseminating information has transformed industrial, political, and cultural practices and processes. Manufacturing, elections, and creative efforts are increasingly dependent on informational inputs. This has conferred great value on some categories of information. The production and sale of information have become major sites of profit making. What had been in large measure a social good has been transformed into a commodity for sale.

Wherever potentially profitable information is produced, the drive for its commercialization rapidly follows. In the scientific sector, for example, research findings have become a source of intense effort to gain competitive advantage. Profit-seeking ventures now penetrate the core of many major universities and threaten to undermine the openness of the scholarly community.

Science, the publication of the American Association for the Advancement of Science (AAAS), increasingly publishes accounts of distinguished scientists engaged in deal making, organizing their own companies, or selling their findings to existing enterprises. A more and more typical report observes: "In many areas of biology these days it's hard to find a researcher who doesn't hold biotech equity (in a for-profit company)."[7] The University of Miami's vice president for research voiced concern over this condition:

> As money becomes less and less available, more people are going to be compromising their principles, compromising their time . . . We can get to the point at some stage in this process where we're not research universities any longer but fee-for-service corporations—hired guns.[8]

No less emphatic in his disapproval of these developments, Derek Bok, as reported in the *Chronicle of Higher Education*, in his final "President's Report" to Harvard's Board of Overseers, found "the commercialization of universities as (perhaps) the most severe threat facing higher education." Harvard's former president said: "[Universities] appear less and less as a charitable institution seeking truth and serving students and more and more, as a huge commercial operation that differs from corporations only because there are no shareholders and no dividends."[9]

This distinction, too, may be rapidly disappearing. In mid-1993, Harvard Medical School announced its intention to invite the Healthcare Investment Corporation, "the largest venture capital firm in the biotechnology field," to "share facilities in a new building." More than this, the site will be filled "with companies that intend to turn Harvard science into health care products by working closely with the research teams and even financing some of them, with Harvard holding the patents and the companies paying licensing fees . . ."[10]

The ties between university researchers and private corporations have grown so close that the Director of the Food and Drug Administration felt compelled to issue a statement in 1994: "There is a growing recognition in the academic and scientific communities that certain financial arrangements between clinical investigators and product sponsors, or the personal financial interests of clinical investigators and product sponsors, can potentially bias the outcome of clinical trials."[11] In brief, research itself may be contaminated by these increasingly institutionalized arrangements.

The commercial incursion is not limited to universities. The single largest generator of new information, produced in pursuit of its public functions, is the United States Government. Not surprisingly, the rich informational pool derived from governmentally undertaken and financed activity has been an early target for corporate takeover. In the last fifteen years it has been enveloped in market relationships, its contents commercialized, and its disposition privatized. Its widespread general availability, formerly under-written by public taxation, has been progressively narrowed and subjected to the criterion of ability to pay.

Government information has been steadily siphoned off into commercial products, where it has not been eliminated entirely. The American Library Association called attention to this phenomenon early on and has continued to voice its concern. In the most recent edition of its fourteen-year old chronology, "Less Access to Less Information By and About the U.S. Government," it continues to document the multiplying efforts to restrict and commercialize government information. At the same time, some government holdings have been made more accessible by electronic distribution. How long this will endure without fees and charges being introduced is an open question.[12] The practice of selling governmental (or any) information, serves the corporate user well. Ordinary individual users go to the end of the dissemination queue. Profoundly antidemocratic in its effect, privatizing and/or selling information, which at one time was considered public property, has become a standard practice in recent years.

A subset of the wider phenomenon has been the behavior of political leaders who leave office. U.S. District Court Judge Charles A. Richey ruled in a 1975 decision "that [documents and other informational matter] . . . produced or kept by a public official in the administration and performance of the powers and duties of a public office belong to the government and may not be considered the property of the official." But his ruling to date has been mostly ignored.[13]

Nearly twenty years after the Richey ruling, the *New York Times* editorialized after the November 1992 elections: "Over the years, Presidents have managed to establish legal claim to their papers chiefly because they possessed them when they left office. Rather than fight with departing Presidents, Federal officials negotiated for limited access."[14] Under this perverse procedure, former President Richard Nixon sued, and was upheld by a U.S. District Court of Appeals for compensation for the White House tapes and papers that were seized when he was the subject of the Watergate scandal.[15]

Withholding public documentation for private gain is not limited to former Presidents. Innumerable other former high governmental officials have taken personal possession of papers associated with their public service. Cavalierly regarding public documents as private property, the material has been used for financial gain in the sale of personal memoirs and historical studies.

There is still another factor, in addition to greed, that has limited and mis-shapen what should be the public record. The Bush Administration, for example, destroyed vital information to prevent it from coming into the possession of its successor. Federal archivists reported many computer tapes were missing from the White House computer record.[16] Upon assuming office, the Clinton Administration did nothing to preserve the Bush computer record. Actually, the Administration was excoriated by, once again, Judge Richey, for its dilatory behavior. "This case has been one of avoidance of responsibiity by the government bureaucracy."[17] The Clinton Administration contested Richey's ruling, but it was upheld by the U.S. Court of Appeals for the District of Columbia.[18] Whether the Government will appeal further or abide by the Appeals Court decision and take measures to safeguard for archival use its own electronics communications is, as this book goes to press, uncertain.

The commercialization and privatization of government and scientific information has become a paradox. Unarguably, it has been of great benefit to affluent users who now have access to kinds and amounts of data that would have been unimaginable only a few years ago. Commercialization therefore has been rewarding to private information providers and to their clients. For the rest of the population, the vast majority, the quality and the availability of information leaves a lot to be desired. In the domain of general governmental information, the supply has been curtailed severely. The American Library Association notes that "since 1982, one of every four of the Government's 16,000 publications has been eliminated."[19]

The National Security State and Information

While commercialization and privatization of information have been steadily encroaching on the public's information supply, the information policies of the National Security State have exacted a still heavier toll on the public's access to the vital information over most of the twentieth century, especially the last fifty years of Cold War. As the Cold War has subsided—though not entirely disappeared—some of its effects on the national information condition have begun to be noted and tentative steps taken to change decades-old policies. The National Archives, for example, "has estimated it has 300 million to 400 million classified documents dating from the World War I era to the mid-1950s. Countless other documents are housed at other Government agencies."[20] The Pentagon, the CIA, and the State Department are three major storehouses of long-term and current classified information.

Another agency with an overflowing stockpile of such material is the Department of Energy, the national keeper of nuclear arms and nuclear programs. The Department of Energy, according to its Secretary, possesses "at least thirty-two million pages of secret papers." This still-secret hoard is given this appreciation by Mrs. O'Leary, the Energy Department's Secretary: "it's thirty-two Washington Monuments. . . it's three miles worth of data."[21] Its real significance—the impact of nuclear tests and released radiation, the existence and extent of toxic waste sites, unexamined government-corporate deals, and so on—can hardly be represented by physical measurements of the documentation.[21]

Beyond the withholding of vast amounts of information, much of it deserving to be known by the public but much of it of questionable value to anyone, the massive classification of data for "national security" has had an appalling effect on American society since the end of the Second World War. It has served to create a general climate of secrecy and acted as a deterrent to public discussion of countless political issues that deserved widespread airing, rather than airtight suppression.

In 1994, indicative of the continuing, though unacknowledged, economic crisis, the Government acted to revise and loosen some of its classification procedures. A Pentagon-CIA study on security classification of documents estimated the costs of maintaining an extensive system of security management as "more than $14 billion a year in the private sector alone."[22] One unexpected benefit of the economic crunch, therefore, may be the financial inability of the Government's coercive centers to continue to put as much documentation as they would like under lock and key. But unbridled enthusiasm that the country is on its way to general information declassification is not yet warranted. Though President Clinton ordered millions of documents declassified in 1994 and extended the order in 1995 to all secret documents more than twenty-five years old, the chief defenders of secrecy, the CIA, the Pentagon, and the State Department continue to resist complying.[23]

Varieties of Privatization: Contracting Out

There is more to the problem of making public information widely available than the obstacles raised by its commercialization and governmental secrecy, important as these are. The advance of privatization into more and more governmental activities has taken different forms. One of the most widespread, and whose effects are still to be fully calculated, is what is called "contracting out." In this arrangement, government at any level— local, state, or national—makes deals to have some of its functions undertaken by private contractors. As has been described in Chapter 2, this is essentially the direction that public school management is taking.

Justified to the public as a significant money-saving strategy and as a means of reducing the role of government—a central tenet of conservative doctrine for a very long time, particularly pronounced in the Reagan years, and infused with new vigor in the 104th Congress—contracting, or "outsourcing," has been a flourishing field in Washington, and elsewhere around the country. It has been widely adopted for all kinds of what were once public services—fire protection, waste disposal, some elements of the judicial system, libraries, and even policing. According to a statement of the U.S. General Accounting Office, "civilian agencies currently spend about $55 billion per year on contracts and have become increasingly dependent on contractors to help agencies manage and carry out their missions."[24] In some government agencies, for example, the Department of Energy, the Environmental Protection Agency, and the National Aeronautics and Space Administration, "contractors are performing virtually all of the work."[25]

In addition to the colossal waste found to exist in the general practice of contracting out governmental information functions (see OMB report[24]), there are related problems that seriously affect the national information supply, especially the needs of the general citizenry. The American Library Association describes one of these problems: "The increased emergence of contractual agreements with commercial firms to disseminate information collected at taxpayer expense, [has resulted in] higher user charges for government information and the proliferation of government information in electronic format only."[26] In each case, the individual, ordinary user is disadvantaged.

Still more problematic, when the information function is transferred from governmental oversight, criteria other than public interest may determine the formats, organization, and categories of the information produced. What may be of importance to the general user may be of little concern to largescale commercial users. When the supply function is commercialized, the priority inevitably goes to the major paying customers. When this occurs, what may be missing is not even realized. If the collection and organization process is exclusionary at the outset, data absence may not be recognized. But visible or not, deprivation exists.

The reliance on private firms to do what once was the government's work, via contracting out, has grown markedly in recent years in keeping with the conservative philosophy of abandoning the protective social role of Government. It has had especially damaging effects on the public information supply. The Office of Management and Budget (OMB) noted that despite the huge sums involved in the private contracting sphere, information about the management of the projects was sadly missing. Auditors were in short supply and as of the end of 1992, $160 billion in contracts had not been audited. In short, no one knew how the taxpayers' money had been spent, although there were enough clues to indicate that the waste was staggering.[27]

Contracting out governmental activities to private enterprise has created a vast black hole in information about the government's essential functions. Yet it is only part of the story of a growing deficiency in such information. When public business is removed from government management, under its new private managers, it is likely to become less transparent to the public.

This condition has been widened and institutionalized by the wave of deregulation that has swept over the nation since the mid-1970s. Whether these practices will be reversed in the years ahead remains to be seen, though the trends are hardly reassuring. What can be safely said at this time, is that the damage to public information is already severe, its full dimensions still largely unknown, and its impact likely to be long-lasting.

Deregulation

Actually, deregulation of industry in the United States predates the 1970s. It began to appear, in limited ways, as early as the Eisenhower era (1952–1960). The New Deal measures, initiated in the 1930s, began to be rolled back by a resurgent corporate sector, enriched and reinvigorated by the massive military outlays required for waging World War II, as well as the immediate postwar recovery expenditures. In this period, American Big Business concentrated its energies on consolidating its hold on the domestic economy and expanding into a wide-open European and global market. The regulations imposed in the Roosevelt era, though never acceptable to Big Business, were borne relatively easily while the economy grew rapidly at home and abroad. American products and services, for two decades, filled the global shelves. The U.S. dollar was the global currency.

Relatively quickly however, the Western European and Japanese economies gained strength and the bite of their competition into American business' profitability began to be felt. The immediate corporate reaction at home was to focus on regulation as the chief source of its problem. "By the late 1970s," two Washington journalists reported, "complaints of excessive regulation had become management's all-purpose cop-out. Were profits too low? Blame regulation. Were prices too high? Blame regulation. Was American industry unable to compete with foreign competition? Blame regulation."[28]

Besides the ideological value in blaming regulation for the emerging business difficulties in the '70s, substantial material objectives also were served. In the communication sector this was particularly evident. Writer Jeremy Tunstall explained the growing pressure for deregulation as one means to hold on to the U.S.' world hegemonic position:

> Behind the loose deregulatory consensus lie the twin assumptions that communication is becoming the number one industry in the world, and that the traditional position of the U.S. as numero uno in all aspects of electronics/telecommunications/video/entertainment/computers/information technology is being challenged. A central purpose [of deregulation of communications] is to maintain both communications and the U.S. as number one.[29]

Tunstall also observed that "American business had geared itself up much more systematically in the last decade [1970–1980] to influence politics," through lobbying and the use of the mass media.[30]

Tunstall's perceptions were well grounded. With almost unlimited access to the domestic information system—actually it owned it—American Big Business moved decisively, with the communication sector in the forefront, to get rid of whatever rules they regarded as impediments to management autonomy and profit making. Primarily, aim was taken at the social functions of Government that had been strengthened in the Roosevelt period and expanded in the brief Great Society years of Lyndon Johnson, which lasted only from the mid-1960s to the early 70s. "The prime targets," the aforementioned Washington reporters noted, "were those agencies that sought to protect consumers and workers and to improve the air, water, and workplace. They were the agencies, in effect, that tried to get industry off the backs of the people."[31]

Another target was the Federal Communications Commission (FCC), with its mandate to oversee the vital and powerful communications sector. It too, had to be "reined in," though anyone familiar with the industry-serving commission had to regard its alleged role as a protector of the public interest, and a scourge of the broadcasters, as a fantasy.

In any case, reducing or eliminating the social regulatory function over consumer and workplace protection and corporate communication practices, also meant reducing or eliminating public information about these crucial social spheres. When industry is relieved of certain democratic obligations to pay its share of taxes, control pollution, reduce toxic wastes, cease interfering with work place rights of the labor force, provide adequate children's and public affairs TV programming, the data concerning these social undertakings either vanishes or never gets collected. In short, data vital to social well-being silently falls out of the national information supply, its absence noted, if at all, only when some later potential user finds it no longer exists or never was generated.

Indicative of what now may be a pervasive condition was the experience of the Task Force on National Health Care Reform, established in the first days of the then newly-elected Clinton Administration. In formulating its proposals, it encountered an unexpected difficulty: it could not find basic data. The *New York Times* reported that the Task Force "discovered that the Government quit collecting state-by-state data on health spending a decade ago. The Federal Government tabulated health spending by state from 1966 through 1982, but has not compiled state data since then . . ."[32] What this account does *not* say is that this data gap originated with the many data discontinuances ordered by the Reagan White House in its zeal to cut out the social functions of government. As this kind of data apparently was of little interest to commercial vendors and their corporate clientele, it just "disappeared," like critics in Argentina or Chile in the 1970s.

Another especially egregious example of withholding data has been the unconscionable suppression by knowledgable corporate tobacco management, for two decades, of research findings revealing the linkage of smoking to cancer. With no obligation to provide its internally generated information to a public regulatory authority, a generation of citizens' health has been sacrificed to the sovereign law of proprietary information.[33]

The absence of health and human welfare data as a consequence of deregulated corporate activity, directly affects the well-being of the entire population. Less vital, though hardly inconsequential, are gaps in economic information that may cause large numbers of people substantial loss. For example, a pitifully inadequate oversight staff in the Securities and Exchange Commission can hardly cope with the potential for financial malpractice in the enormous mutual funds industry. Here is an account of the current condition of oversight in this industry. "What tools are available," asks a reporter, "to mutual fund regulators for monitoring America's rapidly growing . . . industry? Pitifully few." This for an industry of 4,900 firms and more than $2 trillion of Americans' savings. The information offered investors is often bland or impenetrable legalese. It is an industry seriously undermonitored and thereby potentially waiting for a debacle.[34]

Paradoxically, accompanying the shortfall of social welfare, human care, and economic information essential to the well-being of the majority is an enormously enlarged amount of custom-tailored information priced for an upscale clientele and thereby available to commercial and corporate users, or whoever can afford to pay for it. The information needs of the corporate sector, to the most minute and refined degree, are now satisfied instantaneously. What is occurring in the information sphere is of a piece with what can be observed in the economy at large. The social order is splitting into at least a two-tiered structure, one with a full and expanding range of social and economic amenities; the other with a declining share of both, but also with a growing amount of junk food, junk entertainment, and junk information.

Finally, deregulation in the communication sphere, in addition to encouraging a more rapid concentration of facilities—radio, TV, cable, and press—in fewer and fewer hands, also enables the newer media, especially cable, to claim First Amendment rights. When and if these rights are conferred, the now heavily concentrated cable franchise owners (MCOs, multiple cable owners) will be able, among other benefits, to avoid their obligation to provide public access channels in the communities they serve. Their argument is that they are being deprived of their free speech if government insists that they make some of their channels available for public purposes. This is a development to watch for in the future.

The Current Scene

In sum, the last fifty years have witnessed a phenomenal growth of corporate power deployed across the social and economic landscape. The expansion of this power has relied heavily on three far-reaching structural
changes in the institutional infrastructure: deregulation of economic activity, privatization of functions once public, and commercialization of activities once social.

Taken together and applied to the now-central sector of communication
and information, the impact of these processes is profoundly altering the informational condition and the democratic character of American society.
The corporate voice is the loudest in the land. Immense amounts of new information are produced but are available mainly to those who can afford
their costs. The collection of socially vital information has been neglected
or withheld, where it has not been entirely eliminated.

All this has occurred partly as a consequence of a wilful effort to destroy
as much of the social function of government as possible, and as an accom-
paniment of the deregulatory process whereby unsupervised corporate activity leaves few traces of its work. And, not least, public communication,
for the most part, is underwritten and directed by the corporate sector. Independent voices struggle, generally unsuccessfully, to be heard. Economic
activity, politics, and social well-being are either undertaken or evaluated
largely by or with commercial criteria.

Though these developments have been maturing over many decades, the
tempo has accelerated in the last fifteen or so years, reaching a crescendo
with the election and early legislative activity of the 104th Congress in
1995. However conservative the character of this body, it is the inevitable
outcome of the direction corporate power has chosen to take since the end
of the Second World War. The unwavering and persistent objectives of the
business system over this period have been to extend its authority, while at
the same time narrowing that of the national government's, particularly its
social function. Newt Gingrich and his supporters in and outside the Congress may sound like wild men to those who grew up with New Deal or
Great Society expectations. Yet their conservative credo that regards government responsibility for national welfare as a blueprint of socialism is
only the most recent expression of the same message that has been financed
by Big Business and disseminated through their corporate media and entertainment channels for decades.[35]

And so, despite the impressive capabilities of the new information technologies and the proliferation of electronic informational networks, there is
little likelihood that the data deficit of social information will soon disap-
pear. The new informational networks more likely will be absorbed into the
commercial cocoon that has engulfed most of society's activities. The In-

ternet itself is not exempt from the powerful commercializing and for-profit currents flowing nationally and internationally. Plans and moves to commercialize the Internet already exist and may be expected to be implemented in the time ahead. With the perspectives and approaches now in command in Washington, and throughout the country, the crisis in American information and communication can only deepen.

Notes

1. Ben Bagdikian, *The Media Monopoly*, Fourth Edition (Boston: Beacon, 1993).
2. *New York Times*, February 11, 1993, sec. A, p. 11.
3. George Kennan, *Around the Cragged Hill* (New York: W.W. Norton, 1993), p. 167.
4. Peter Applebome, "Adman in Atlanta Tries to Sell City," *New York Times*, February 9, 1993, sec. A, p. 8.
5. Kennan, op. cit. p. 167.
6. Bill McKibben, *The Age of Missing Information* (New York: Random House, 1992), p. 236.
7. Marcia Barinaga, "Confusion on the Cutting Edge," *Science* Vol. 257, July 31, 1992, pp. 616–619. Also, "Hughes' Tough Stand on Industry Ties," *Science*, Vol. 259 (February 12, 1993), pp. 884–889.
8. Anthony De Palma, "Universities' Reliance on Companies Raises Vexing Questions in Research," *New York Times*, March 17, 1993, Sec. B, p. 8.
9. Liz McMillen, "Quest for Profits May Damage Basic Values of Universities, Harvard's Bok Warns," *Chronicle of Higher Education*, Number 32, April 24, 1991, p. 1.
10. Susan Diesenhouse, "Harvard's New Test-Tube Business," *New York Times*, August 22, 1993.
11. Stephen Burd, "FDA Seeks Disclosure of Companies' Financial Ties to Researchers," *Chronicle of Higher Education*, October 5, 1994, sec. A, p. 28.
12. "Less Access To Less Information By and About the U.S. Government: XXII, A 1994 Chronology: January–June," American Library Association, Washington, D.C., bi-annual, June 1994.
13. "Richard M. Nixon v. Arthur F. Sampson, Government Records Are Public Property," Advertisement in *New York Times*, June 2, 1993, Sec. A, p. 13.
14. "Richard Nixon's Unjust Demand," Editorial, *New York Times*, November 19, 1992.
15. "Court Says Nixon Must Be Compensated for Tapes," *New York Times*, November 18, 1982.
16. John O'Neill, "Bush Tapes Lost, U.S. Archivists Say," *New York Times*, March 14, 1993, p. 16.
17. "Judge Calls Administration Lax on Predecessors' Computer Records," *New York Times*, June 9, 1993, p. 8.
18. Neil A. Lewis, "Government Told to Save Messages Sent by Computer," *New York Times*, August 14, 1993, p. 1.
19. "Less Access to Less Information", op. cit.

20. Neil A. Lewis, "A Debate Rages Over Disclosure of U.S. Secrets," *New York Times*, January 14, 1994, sec. A, p. 11.
21. William J. Broad, "U.S. Begins Effort to Recast the Law on Atomic Secrets," *New York Times*, January 9, 1994, p. 1.
22. Tim Weiner, "Bills Seek to Slash the Number of U.S. Secrets," *New York Times*, March 3, 1994.
23. Tim Weiner, "Some Spying Secrets Will Stay Out in the Cold," *New York Times*, February 18, 1995, sec. 4, p. 3.
24. Statement of J. Dexter Peach before the Subcommittee on Oversight and Investigations, Committee on Energy and Commerce, House of Representatives, December 3, 1992. GAO Report, "Federal Contracting," GAO/T-RCED-93-2.
25. Keith Schneider, "U.S. Lack of Supervision Encouraged Waste in Contracts," *New York Times*, December 2, 1992, p. 1.
26. "Less Access to Less Information, op. cit.
27. Schneider, op. cit.
28. Susan Tolchin and Martin Tolchin, *Dismantling America*, (Boston: Houghton Mifflin, 1983), pp.4-5.
29. Jeremy Tunstall, *Communication Deregulation*, (Oxford: Basil Blackwell, 1986), p. 7.
30. *Ibid*, p. 12.
31. Tolchin and Tolchin, op. cit. pp. 39–40
32. Robert Pear, "Health Data Sought by Clinton is No Longer Collected," *New York Times*, March 1, 1993, sec. A, p. 13.
33. Philip J. Hilts, "Cigarette Makers Debated the Risks They Denied," and, "Tobacco Maker Studied Risk But Did Little About Results," *New York Times*, June 16, 1994, p. 1, and June 17, 1994, p. 1.
34. Diana B. Henriques, "Seeking Data on Funds, Investors and Regulators Find Frustration," *New York Times*, August 9, 1994, sec. A, p. 1.
35. "Gingrich Denounces Editorial 'Socialists'," *New York Times*, March 9, 1995, sec. A, p. 9.

4

SPECIAL EFFECTS: MEDIA HIGH TECH FOR CAPTURING VIEWERS

Special Effects: Media High Tech for Capturing Viewers

Social information deficit notwithstanding, the U.S. media-informational sphere enjoys an uncontested, and still growing, global primacy. This is true despite the equally striking fact that communication in America has been nearly totally appropriated for a sole objective: marketing—marketing of goods, services, political outlooks and candidates, ideas, emotional release, or what have you. This relationship—a powerful media apparatus linked tightly to salesmanship—creates a general condition that in time threatens the viability, and sustainability, of society. How and why is this apocalyptic prospect unfolding?

The starting point is the nature of the American market in the years after World War II and some of the major developments that have affected it; e.g., war, the militarization of science, and the emergence of a transnational business system that seeks ever more powerful ways to sell goods and its own legitimacy.

The Market in the Postwar Years

The United States was a powerful producer of consumer goods *before* World War II, leaving aside the drastic drop in production during the Great Depression of the 1930s. In the war, the American industrial machine, unmatched at the time, concentrated on production of war goods: tanks, munitions, aircraft, military supplies. But the Depression remained a vivid memory and few would have predicted the continued expansion of industry that followed hostilities. Many, in fact, remained anxious that the economy would recede into the prewar economic crisis.

Withal, the deferred domestic demand and the forced savings (e.g., war bonds) that accumulated during the war years pushed postwar output in

America to unprecedented levels. To this was added the orders that replenished Europe, stripped bare during the Nazi Occupation. Accordingly, the industrial plant built during the war and later converted to civilian production, supplemented with massive capital investment and expansion of industrial capacity in the early postwar years, provided a powerful productive base. From it flowed a huge volume of consumer goods in the late 1940s, '50s, and '60s. Eric Hobsbawm, in his masterful history of the twentieth century, sees this relatively brief period as "the golden years" of capitalism.[1]

The ability of Americans to buy these goods kept up with their output, at least until the early 1970s. United States personal consumption expenditures (in constant 1982 dollars), fueled by hot and cold wars of the period (Korea, Vietnam, the Cold War over four decades), rose from $503 billion in 1940 to $2,682 billion in 1990, a five-fold increase over the fifty year interval, while the population roughly doubled in size in the same period. By decade, the percentage increase in personal consumption expenditures was: 1940–1950, 46%; 1950–1960, 37%; 1960–1970, 49%; 1970–1980, 34%; and 1980–1990, 34%.[2]

The income to sustain these rapidly rising expenditures was heavily supplemented with the growth of the credit industry, which discovered all kinds of imaginative ways to induce the assumption of staggering personal debt burdens. Completing the infrastructure of the consumer society in-the-making was the parallel expansion of the advertising industry and advertising expenditures over the period.

The advertising industry has been the chosen instrument of the unplanned, yet heavily concentrated American economy, to clear the inventory off the corporate shelves. At the same time, as a special bonus, it also supplies strong and pervasive doses of dreams and myths that sustain the governing order. This is more flatteringly expressed by advertising authority Robert Coen:

> Unlike the European societies, the U.S. had no established rigid marketing system, guilds or hierarchies, and U.S. entrepreneurs were not constrained in developing their enterprises. They discovered that they would prosper if they spread the word about their goods and services. The advertising industry, as known today, has mainly evolved from the American experience.[3]

It is precisely on account of the fact that American businessmen, historically, have had fewer constraints, that the model of economic development in its purest capitalist form was constructed in the United States. In that model, advertising occupies a central position. It is to be expected and, in fact, is confirmed, that "in the case of advertising, most of the advanced developments have occurred first in the United States."[4] This continues to be the situation today.

For advertising to fulfill its systemically crucial role—getting the national output of goods and services into the hands and homes of buyers and reaffirming daily, if not hourly, that consumption is the definition of democracy—it must have full access to the nation's message-making and -transmitting apparatus. Over time, this means the transformation of the press, radio, television, cable, the satellite, and now, the computer, into instrumentations of marketing.

The corporate economy has done this with singleminded devotion, and has succeeded so well that the nation's image and message-making machinery has been almost fully directed to salesmanship. The press is dependent on advertising for approximately three-quarters of its income. Radio and television, excluding the public channels, which reach only a tiny slice of the national audience, are totally reliant on advertising revenues. As each new medium has appeared, it has drained off some of the marketing income. Broadcast television and cable television are now the primary, though by no means exclusive, vehicles for the sales message.

All this is well known, amply documented and analyzed in the trade and academic literature. What the record reveals is an almost total takeover of the domestic informational system for the purpose of selling goods, services, people, and prefabricated opinion. What is not so familiar, however, is the extent to which the marketing function has influenced the form and shaped the content of the new information technologies to suit its purpose. This can be appreciated best by reviewing the history of the new information technologies since the Second World War.

War and Business: Recent Stimulants to Technological Development

The production of imagery and messages relies on institutional structures and relationships as well as instrumentation. The end product is the result of a complex interaction of processes, techniques, and social relationships in constant flux, with changing weights for each component. The American message and image machine, responding mostly to two separate but related forces, military and corporate, has developed special features over the last half-century.

Henry Luce's *American Century,* a corporate vision revealed in 1941, was a design thoroughly dependent on a greatly expanded international network of communication. It also foretold of armed forces in place around the globe to defend the emerging system of American economic power and ideological persuasion.[5] When the Cold War ended in the early 1990s, "the United States had 375 foreign military installations staffed by more than 500,000 servicemen and women worldwide."[6]

America also had a powerful scientific and technological establishment that was created in World War II and expanded in the postwar years. This decisive element of national power was the offspring of the astronomical Cold War budget that channelled massive funds into scientific research and development for more than forty years. These sums poured into federal and corporate laboratories and academic and private installations. A science reporter assessed the effects of these expenditures:

> By some measures, the cold war was the best thing that ever happened to research. The explosion of money, talent and tools far exceeded anything in previous eras . . . over the decades [an] army of government, academic and industry experts made the breakthroughs that gave the West its dazzling military edge . . . Since 1955, the Government has spent more than *$1 trillion* on research and development of nuclear arms and other weaponry.

From this almost inconceivably large outlay came, among other products, laser weapons, spy satellites, precision armaments, weather satellites, computer chips, in fact "the whole industries of aerospace, communications and electronics . . ."[7] And out of this proliferation of scientific and technological projects of military and corporate parentage has come what is reassuringly called the Information Society. We are now living, we are informed, in the Information Age. Yet the main beneficiaries of the new capabilities in information production, transmission, and dissemination, not unexpectedly, are those who were the main initiating agents of the Cold War era, foremost among whom are the transnational companies, the intelligence, military, and policing agencies.

Especially well rewarded were the big businesses with worldwide operations. With their new facilities they have the means to manage global activities, move capital, shift production locales, and, on the basis of these new capabilities, weaken organized labor and national oversight authority. At the same time, the Pentagon and the intelligence agencies built intercontinental satellite networks for communicating with their worldwide installations, for monitoring the flow of messages of friends and foes alike, and for mapping the world for possible future interventions, e.g., Libya, North Korea, Cuba, inner-city Detroit, Los Angeles.

While this new technological capability might have been expected to strengthen and perpetuate American domination of the international realm—and for a brief time it did—other developments intervened to erode U.S. national power; for one, the war in Vietnam. In recent years the growth of rival industrial systems in Germany, Japan, and South East Asia has further diminished American influence around the world. *But not in all sectors.* And especially not in the increasingly central sphere of communication.

The new information technologies enhanced the vigor and production quality of the American cultural industries—radio, television, film, publishing, et al.—conferring on them a marked technical edge. But this was no random transfer of technical expertise. A familiar and pervasive force—the marketing imperative—initiated and guided the adaptation of many of the new technological processes into the cultural industries. The process responded closely to the growing pressures on the overall American economy.

In the first postwar decades, there was scant need for American marketers to take into account either the domestic or the global buyers' tastes and preferences. American goods had few competitors. The early postwar boom years enabled U.S. products to be marketed with effective but unexceptional advertising, though the advent of television provided the merchandiser with a new and extraordinary instrument for salesmanship. American media products were pumped into the world market with few constraints.

These "good times" for American industry began to falter in the late 1960s. Though at first a seemingly temporary irritant, the pressure on the economy of renewed foreign industrial competition, along with the exhaustion of the postwar replenishment boom, continued to build. In the late 1980s and early 1990s it became relentless. The faltering of industrial production, so observable domestically, was occurring as well across most of the industrialized world.

New Means for Bolstering the Marketing Message: The Emergence of the Special Effects Industry

The marketing imperative took on a new urgency in the 1970s as the search for consumers became increasingly feverish. Messages addressed to potential consumers multiplied and intensified. As the overall U.S. power position deteriorated, its one sphere of unchallenged mastery, media-driven culture, received mounting dosages of adrenalin from technologies and processes developed originally to serve the empire. Now they were aimed at producing consumers. Popular culture fused with merchandising, adapting and employing the instrumentation and techniques that appeared earlier in the research labs of the cold and corporate warriors.

Indeed, an entirely new economic sphere emerged, the special effects industry, difficult as it is to place into the standard industrial classification. What, for example, is the product of a Hollywood shop, aptly called *Industrial Light and Magic*, George Lucas' commercial special effects company? Yet it is not some hidden or mysterious sphere. As the screen credits for *Dick Tracy* or *The Mask*, for example, unfold, a battalion of names appears in one or another highly specialized fields, generically considered "special effects."

Industrial Light and Magic was one of the first in the field. It no longer enjoys its former near-monopoly position. New companies, as well as in-house divisions in the big electronic-pop cultural conglomerates (e.g., Sony, Disney, Time Warner, have become indispensable collaborators with the TV, video, recording, TV-game, and interactive media production forces. A report on a recently-formed special effects company, *Digital Domain,* 50% owned by IBM, noted that "The special effects arena once was a highly specialized niche . . . but now it is exploding."[8] Participating in the explosion, Disney has set up *Image Works,* and Sony has announced the creation of an in-house special effects company.[9]

The use of special effects long precedes the current period. They were certainly evident in the early development of film. But the elevation of special effects into a primary constituent of film and general entertainment is much more recent. It can probably (and arbitrarily) be assigned to their use in *Star Wars,* produced in 1977. A case also can be made for Stanley Kubrick's *2001*; when it was made in 1970 it achieved a startling pseudo-environment.

The actual date that marks the full emergence and use of special effects in the cultural industries is uncertain. It is sufficient to note that sometime in the post–World War II period, centered in the late '60s and early '70s, the provision of special effects became a powerful and observable component of popular cultural forms and products. Though no one factor explains this development, and several have believability, it is my contention that *one contributing stimulus stands out. It is the intensifying sales effort to maintain and extend market share at home and abroad.*

In a word, the big United States consumer-goods producers, a.k.a. "the national sponsors," and their advertising agencies have been pressing unremittingly to target audiences/consumers with ever more powerful sales messages. It is probably true that this many-pronged effort would have been undertaken routinely in the day-in-day-out operations of corporate businesses, as they continuously jostle for market share. But the additional pressure, and the time in which it becomes manifest, coincides with the onset of fierce global industrial competition and creeping domestic economic stagnation.

Conveniently, thanks to trillion-dollar R and D (research and development) expenditures, a constellation of new techniques and technologies—some applied in other uses—were invented to satisfy the most extravagant expectations of corporate marketers and salesmen. These technical capabilities for use in visual, optical, photographic, and audio forms, offered improved ways to intensify excitement, organize audience attention, and capture and hold interest. What better describes the objectives of advertisers on behalf of their sponsors, or record producers, hoping for platinum disc sales, or movie producers seeking box-office blockbusters? The special effects industry is an extraordinarily acquisitive and derivative industry that actively searches out advanced technologies from elsewhere—the sciences, medicine, computer graphics, personal computer developments—and puts them to astonishing use.

In a related way, the marketing effort was applied as well to stimulating personal acquisition of a growing number of electronics products that became available about the same time. This served, conveniently, to make existing record collections and record players for example, obsolete. The introduction of personal computers on a mass scale, the phenomenal popular embrace of VCRs and the promotion of compact discs (CDs) opened up new consumer markets and launched new entertainment products.

These new electronic goods also enabled individuals to draw spectacular techniques into their own living rooms. Looming now is High Definition TV (HDTV). HDTV, when and if it is introduced, promises to make America's existing stock of television sets (hundreds of millions) instantaneously out-of-date. This is obsolescence, planned or not, with a vengeance. Oddly enough, HDTV may be obsolete itself *before* it reaches the stage of large-scale installation. Enhanced computers for multimedia use may totally bypass HDTV.

And so it has developed. In recent years, TV commercials, movies, TV programs, and recordings increasingly have called upon special effects to rivet an audience's attention. Special effects sound and imagery short circuit the brain and hit the gut. Content recedes and reflection disappears as technique flourishes. This may be the defining feature of what is called postmodernity.

George Lucas, the pre-eminent special effects creator and entrepreneur, understandably sees extravagant promise in the field:

> We see the world of special effects and the world of production moving into one entity . . . It changes the production process. Writers have been restricted in the way they think by what they think is possible.[10]

Computer technology, in Lucas' view, will unshackle hitherto hobbled creative talent. Yet the results to date, of applying computer wizardry to film, television and artistic effort in general, contradict Lucas' claim. The very opposite seems to be occurring. The utilization of special effects, especially those of the most recent vintage, seems to lead to a *reduction* in the creative substance of the project.

Jurassic Park, possibly the greatest achievement of special effects in a film to date, is an exemplary case in point. Reviewing the show, the *Los Angeles Times* film critic wrote:

> Do the Dinosaurs Work? Indeed they do. Does anything else? Not really. . .
> some six kinds of dinosaurs come to life with a verisimilitude that is humbling and that also blends seamlessly with the film's considerably blander and less

interesting human characters . . . Spielberg has chosen to make an amusement park instead of a motion picture.[11]

This could be interpreted as one critic's complaint. It was, however, the reaction of most reviewers. More to the point, it is not a question of special effects in *one* movie. It is a general trend *across the culture*, to substitute visual imagery and sound and motion for content and substance.

Philip Hayward writes about these developments in music video and MTV where he sees "the impact of special effects as stimulating and retaining audiences," and bypassing "concern with textual profundity in favor of technological 'magic,' and rewarding highly competitive forces."[12] More pointedly still, another writer sees the ultimate effect of special effects techniques in pop cultural forms as the triumph of commercialism:

> . . . the wedding of pop music and video has shifted the balance of power between a song and the image of its performer. Where once that image augmented the music, nowadays the music serves the image, which in turn, often serves a fast-food or cola advertising campaign and ultimately a whole line of advertising. Pop stars have always endorsed products, but it has been only in the age of music video that the star image and the product have become indissoluble . . . pop music is no longer a world unto itself but an adjunct of television, whose stream of commercial messages projects a culture in which everything is for sale . . . [and] as the image has taken precedence over the song . . . the songs have become fragmentary and charged with electronic beats . . .[13]

The writer concludes from this that the "wondrous technology" has "tricked us." Yet is this galloping phenomenon merely a matter of smoke and mirrors? More convincing in explaining why this has been happening, I believe, is Martha Rosler's insightful observation that "The confusion of style with substance is fostered by any medium that allows advertising to be integrated into its fabric and format."[14] What Rosler calls attention to is precisely what has been occurring across all media. Advertising, with the full cooperation of the new technologies, has been integrated progressively into film, TV, theatre, recording, and news itself.

In film, for example, the widespread use of the "built-in plug," allows actors to clutch cans of Coke or Bud, or cleaning fluid, seemingly as part of the natural setting. The recent spotlight on the tobacco industry revealed the widespread practice of tobacco companies paying for film scenes of actors smoking:

> Internal memos [of the company] say that Brown & Wiliamson Tobacco Corp. spent more than $950,000 in a span of four years to feature its cigarette brands

in more than twenty movies—including payments of at least $300,000 to ac-
tion film star Sylvester Stallone. The payments took the form of checks, cash,
and merchandise—including jewelry and automobiles . . . [15]

These payoffs were not limited to one tobacco company. Philip Morris and
other corporations engaged in the same game.

Along with selling goods, there are ideological plugs as well. Many
movies, in addition to routinely and endlessly promoting consumption, continue to offer the bromide of rags-to-riches encounters. In these concoc-
tions, attractive but financially distressed young women consort with
humanistic billionaires. These unlikely social workers disinterestedly assist
working (class?) women, e.g., *Batman*, *Pretty Woman*, *Working Girl*.

Television, from its inception, has its drama and sitcom programs written around the commercial break. The climaxes are scheduled carefully either just before or just after the sales message. New technologies enable
imagery to take a giant step beyond this mode of commercialism, widespread as it is.

In recent years, the actual *form* of a presentation is structured for a commercial objective—to hold the viewer/listener captive to the product message. MTV is the purest example of this development and advertising has
appropriated MTV as its own. "'Atmosphere advertising' is the term for ads
driven by music and visuals, with no hard sell . . ."[16] Actually, the MTV network is a continuing, unacknowledged advertisement for musical groups
and record labels. Stuart Ewen points out that "part of the magic formula
embedded in MTV is the fact that viewers [are] looking at an advertisement
without really noticing it."[17] In a *New Yorker* article devoted entirely to
MTV, the writer embellishes this feature: "One of the reasons that MTV is
a landmark in the history of the media is that the boundary between entertainment and advertising has completely disappeared."[18] The impact of
MTV is not limited to TV advertising, important as it is in this domain. It
affects all the media, as well, including print. *USA Today,* for example, offers its news in one or two small paragraphs, print capsules surrounded with
colored copy. The brief sound bites of television news reporting get shorter
each year.

A relatively new MTV news program for young viewers, MTV's basic
audience, boasts *three second interviews* with political figures.[19] As the information gets compacted, so does the general programming. Time com-
pression machines, introduced in the early 1980s, are routinely used to
"make room for more commercials by accelerating the speed of movies and
old television programs." This technique is especially attractive to broadcasters because "The additional minutes of advertising time come without
increased costs for additional programming." With this technique "you can

cut 8% of a two-hour movie by speeding it up [and] gain almost ten minutes without cutting any scenes."[20] What this practice does to the integrity of the original film or TV program does not come into consideration—at least not the consideration of those benefitting from the sale of more commercial time.

The application of special effects to film, TV, and recording to secure viewer/listener attention for a commercial message results inevitably in the evacuation of meaning, other than that of the commercial. A film reviewer writes: "One of the most numbing things about many movies today is how wildly out of scale they seem to go: the way visual and technical virtuosity is juxtaposed with silly, vacuous stories."[21]

The same reviewer reflects further on usage of special effects in film: "There's something dispiriting about the wide disparity in quality between words and images in current American film-making." Writing about a then-current show, *The Lawnmower Man*, it was noted that "Every scene in this cautionary tale about science running amok has spectacular views, unusual camera angles, and moves, or dazzling outré computer effects. And every scene, story-wise, gets mushier and more outlandish or perfunctory . . . ."[22] This could be said about most of the elaborate productions that run up huge budgets. Additionally, special effects techniques are more and more often applied "wall to wall," to sustain the desired sensation throughout the entire film, TV program, or recording, e.g., *Blade Runner*, *Terminator 2*, *Who Framed Roger Rabbit?*, *Jurassic Park*, *Speed*.

Today, the use of special effects to grab the audience's attention has been extended to most other forms of entertainment, regardless of the commercial imperative. That is to say that even where salesmanship of goods is not the primary objective, though sales (of tickets) remains essential, technique rather than substance has prevailed. Perhaps this represents the cultural pollution factor at work.

The condition of the dramatic theater highlights this. Two different drama critics, over a six-month period in 1994, had this to say about the offerings on the New York stage—still the national drama center. In January, *New York Times* critic Vincent Canby headlined his report "Is Broadway Fog-bound in a Special-Effects Age?" He wrote: " . . . the theater is going through—and has been for some time—an escalating evolution in stage trickery roughly equivalent to movies' infatuation with, and emphasis on, ever-more special effects."[23] Five months later, in June, a second major drama critic, David Richards, wrote: " . . . the distinction between Broadway and a theme park grew decidedly narrower during the 1993–94 season . . . [and] theatergoing [has] become an adjunct of tourism, indoor sightseeing.]" Further, " . . . it used to be that spectacle was only a *part* of what Broadway offered its customers. Now it is very nearly everything . . ." Commenting on the Disney theatrical production of *Beauty and the Beast*,

Richards concluded: "*Beauty and the Beast*, whatever its visual appeal, is very nearly content-free."[24]

This inverse relationship between technique and content, increasingly prevalent across all media forms, is the direct outcome of the now-pervasive commercial imperative. If the primary aim of the sponsor, or the producer, is to capture as large an audience as possible for the sales message, or to sell seats, why distract or, worse yet, depress an audience with a serious story line or lyric? Following this logic, the carnival proceeds and the nation's serious business goes unattended, or, attended to, out of sight of the general public.

Export of the American Model

Media-cultural developments in the United States preview their adoption abroad. This occurs in the "normal" course of transacting global business. The expression "world market" now means that globally operating corporations produce and sell their wares in scores of countries. Most of this market is shared by a handful of giant companies in specific spheres—electronics, recordings, cereals, home products, automobiles, pharmaceuticals, and so on. Following this pattern, it is possible to detect, in recent years, a complex unfolding of media, technological, and market relationships across a good part of the world market. It is observable most clearly in Western Europe, Japan, Australia, South Korea, and wherever a national economy has reached a certain level of industrial production.

Each national locale has its own specificities in this evolving pattern, but the common course of development, at least approximately, can be sketched. It runs something like this: Advanced communications technologies have become available. These include computers, satellite communication, broadcast, and cable television. The transnational corporate sector, with its affiliates and dependents *inside* each national configuration, presses for, and succeeds, in achieving what is called "deregulation" or "liberalization" or "privatization." These are variants, which, one way or another, remove national oversight and open the door to commercial utilization of broadcasting and telecommunications. This means financing of TV and cable increasingly by advertising, and the private (corporate) use of telephone lines and computer networks for heavy volume (business) data flows.

With these arrangements in place, the framework is established for the creation and utilization of cultural space in the American mode. And this is the way it has gone! One media-cultural sphere after another has been seized for corporate marketing goals, sometimes by way of media product imports from the U.S., sometimes by imitating American pop cultural production styles, often, a combination of the two. A report on European TV developments is illustrative.

The Hollywood-focused *Los Angeles Times* described a new European TV soap opera, *Riviera*, as having "a decidedly American feel to it." No wonder! The executive producer and creative director of the show were American. "U.S. consultants were hired and brought to Paris for sets, music, lighting and engineering. . . . All taping is done first in English before the show is dubbed into French and other European languages . . . Yet most of the actors, directors, and studio technicians . . . are Europeans . . . [the show was] conceived in a Paris advertising agency."

Why the strong American influence? It derives from the rich historical marketing experience in the U.S. The French producers acknowledge that "The Americans know how to capture and hold an audience. This business can benefit from tricks invented in Hollywood . . . young French writers, [for example] are taught how to structure plots in the American way, which means inserting mini-climaxes before commercial breaks . . . ."[25]

Not only are European TV and film yielding to (welcoming?) the marketing call. The total packaged commercial environment is also becoming familiar. When Disney opened a huge theme park outside Paris in the spring of 1992 *Business Week*, only partly joking, described the imminent event: "And you thought Europe's big happening of 1992 was the creation of a borderless market. The event that really counts is coming April 12. That's when Europe will join the U.S. and Japan as a truly advanced consumer society: It's opening day for Euro-Disneyland." Hyping the Disney opening, "a $6 million newspaper insert, funded partly by corporate partners including Mattel, Coca-Cola, and American Express appeared in seven major cities." *Business Week* asked: "How can Europe resist? Chances are it won't. Cultural imperialism or not, millions of Europeans will soon be careening down Big Thunder Mountain, celebrating the Old World's coming of age."[26]

Actually, Euro-Disney's first two years of operations were a commercial disaster. Whether the expensive playground will be shored up with more Disney capital in the hope that it will gradually become acceptable to European (especially French) audiences, remains to be seen. But what is not in doubt is that there will be continuing waves of transnational corporate capital washing over European, Asian, and Latin American cultural landscapes.

These total communication installations are notably proficient in shepherding the happy throngs who pay for the privilege of being exposed to the commercial messages through artfully integrated and carefully constructed space. In 1988, for instance, MTV European Satellite service was introduced. This network brought together the communication satellite, cable TV, and advanced visual and sonic special effects to transmit the marketing message to an audience in the most effective way. One of the first shows it carried claimed this distinction: "We see *Ultratech* as a very global idea because there is no language, there is no plot, there are no characters . . . It's just sound and light, TV taken down to its essence."[27] In other words, the perfect sales tool!

With deregulation achieved, cable and satellite TV installed, American special effects techniques imported or copied, the Europeans, and many Asians as well, can look forward to world-class (U.S.) levels of commercialism. The international advertising industry is already drooling. "On a per-household basis, four times as much is spent in the United States on television advertising as in Europe . . . the potential for growth in television advertising revenues in Europe is [seen as] enormous . . . the industry still looks like a pot of gold to many."[28]

But is it only gold at the end of the advertising rainbow? Not yet fully visible, but certainly accompanying the short-term profits, is a growing waste of limited natural and human resources. As car sales rise, gas consumption soars, highways circle the earth, and Coke bottles and disposable wrappers lie alongside the road, cultural pollution, too, gushes forth from the global cultural industries.

Autonomous and Neutral Technology?

Calling attention to these developments, it should be emphasized, is not intended to sound yet another antitechnology warning. Technophobia, as Neil Postman would put it, is not the issue.[29] What the evidence here demonstrates is the strong, if not determining, influence of the *original purpose* that fostered the development of each new technology. The social use to which the technology is put, more times than not, follows its originating purpose. When military or commercial advantage are the motivating forces of research and development, it is to be expected that the laboratories will produce findings that are conducive to these objectives. If other motivations could be advanced, the common good, for instance, different technologies might be forthcoming. The customary argument that commerce and profit-seeking go hand-in-hand with social benefit, is still to be demonstrated after hundreds of years of contrary experience.

Kubey and Csikszentmihalyi explain television's alleged *inherent* technological imperative this way:

> This is a good place to debunk the much repeated idea that television is a medium best suited to transmitting emotions, and that it either "cannot" or is not "good" at transmitting ideas . . . The answer to why we see what we see on television lies in a combination of how audiences have come to conceive of the medium, what audiences want to watch (or have grown accustomed to

watching), and what the people who control and sponsor television believe needs to be created and broadcast in order to maximize profit.[30]

Each one of these criteria clearly is a social construct; it is not the outcome of an autonomous technological determinant. The TV that is transmitted, the movies that are made, the music that is recorded and played, and the images that have been photographed and displayed, are increasingly shaped to serve the needs of marketing. This driving force, most pronounced in the United States for many years, is now being experienced in a good part of the rest of the world.

Seemingly, this great success, and the rich returns that flow from it, should be a source of longterm satisfaction and security. Yet a very different reaction is warranted. And herein lies a paradox: a buoyant cultural industry contributing to a looming, though perhaps still distant, social disaster! The media-entertainment industries flourish, their revenues rise, their value to the consumption goods industries continually increases. But the virus of voracious consumerism is embedded in the cultural product that now reaches nearly all corners of the world. The waves of merchandising exhortation carried by, and built into, the popular media, crash against the earth's finite resources.

Whether it be the disposition of atomic wastes, the deepening hole in the ozone layer, or the desperate search for waste disposal sites, underlying each crisis is the misuse of resources. In the fall of 1991 an international group of renowned intellectuals, attending a symposium on "Approaching the Year 2000," noted and indicted the waste and despoiliation of the earth's resources, calling attention to a grotesque distortion in global resource allocation whereby "20% of the world's population consumes 80% of its wealth and is responsible for 75% of its pollution." The source of this shocking phenomenon, the Symposium found, was "the cultural pollution and loss of tradition which have led to global rootlessness, leaving humans, through the intensity of mass-marketing, vulnerable to the pressures of economic and political totalitarianism and habits of mass-consumption and waste which imperil the earth."[31]

The main miscreant in this deepening global crisis is a model of acquisitive behavior and consumerist attitude, constructed and circulated worldwide, by the powerful and deadly combination of media, technology, and the market. Insight into this powerful combination's mechanics found expression in, of all places, a recent personnel announcement of a talent agency. The report stated: "The Creative Artists Agency said today that one of AT&T's highest-ranking executives would join the powerful talent agency in an unexpected move that substantially *advances the convergence of entertainment, information and communications.*" The agency's chief, Michael Ovitz, was more lyrical. He saw the agreement as "the convergence of creativity and communication technology."[32] However the process is described, images and messages today are the outputs of creative talents, using the most advanced information technologies in their production and distribution, for marketing goals.

Notes

1. Eric Hobsbawm, *The Age of Extremes* (New York: Pantheon, 1994.)
2. *Economic Report of the President,* U.S. GPO, Washington, D.C., 1991, p. 303.
3. Robert Coen, "Vast U.S. and Worldwide Ad Expenditures Expected: The Next 20 Years in Advertising and Marketing," *Advertising Age*, November 13, 1980.
4. Coen, *op. cit.*, p. 10.
5. Herbert I. Schiller, *Mass Communications and American Empire*, revised edition (Boulder, CO: Westview Press, 1992 updated edition.) Also (New York: Augustus Kelley, 1969).
6. Joel Brinkley, "U.S. Looking for a Path as a Superpower Conflict Ends," *New York Times*, February 2, 1992, p. 1.
7. William J. Broad, "Swords Have Been Sheathed but Ploughshares Lack Design," *New York Times*, February 5, 1992, sec. A.
8. Jonathan Weber, "IBM Launches Hollywood Special Effects Firm," *Los Angeles Times*, February 26, 1993, sec. D, p. 3.
9. Amy Harmon, "Invasion of the Film Computers," *Los Angeles Times*, August 15, 1993, p. 1.
10. Jonathan Weber, "The Force Is Still With Him," *Los Angeles Times*, April 8, 1993.
11. Kenneth Duran, "Picking Some Big Bones With Jurassic," *Los Angeles Times*, June 11, 1993, sec. F, p. 1.
12. Philip Hayward, editor, *Culture, Technology and Creativity In the Late Twentieth Century* (London: John Libby, 1990), Chapter on "Industrial Light and Magic," p. 128.
13. Stephen Holden, "Strike the Pose: When the Music is Skin-Deep," *New York Times*, August 5, 1990, sec. 2, p. 1.
14. Martha Rosler, "Image Simulations, Computer Manipulations, Some Considerations," *AfterImage*, Vol. 17, No. 4, November 1989, p. 10.
15. Myron Levin, "Tobacco Firm Paid $950,000 to Place Cigarettes in Films," *Los Angeles Times*, May 29, 1994, p. 1.
16. "How MTV Has Rocked Television Commercials," *New York Times*, October 9, 1989.
17. Ibid.
18. John Seabrook, "Rocking in Shangri-La," *New Yorker*, October 16, 1994, p. 69.
19. Karen De Witt, "MTV Puts the Campaign on Fast Forward," *New York Times*, February 8, 1982.
20. Albert Scardino, "TV's Pace and the Ads Increase as Time Goes By," *New York Times*, September 11, 1989, sec. C, p. 10.
21. Michael Wilmington, "Point Break: The Surf Is Up but the Credibility is Down," *Los Angeles Times*, July 1991, sec. F, p. 9.

22. Michael Wilmington, "Science Runs Amok in *Lawnmower Man*," *Los Angeles Times*, March 6, 1992, sec. F., p. 10.
23. Vincent Canby, "Is Broadway Fogbound in a Special-Effects Age?" *New York Times*, January 16, 1994, sec. 2, p. 1.
24. David Richards, "On Stage, Survival of the Fizziest," *New York Times*, June 12, 1994, sec. 2, p. 1. Italics added.
25. Rone Tempest, "Euro-TV Tunes in to Hollywood," *Los Angeles Times*, July 11, 1991, sec. A, p. 1.
26. "Mouse Fever Is About to Strike Europe," *Business Week*, March 20, 1992, p. 32.
27. Jonathan Klein, quoted by Philip Hayward, *op. cit.*
28. Leigh Bruce, "Europeans Tune in to a New Wave of Television," the *International Herald Tribune*, June 11, 1991.
29. Neil Postman, *Technopoly* (New York: Alfred A. Knopf, 1992).
30. Robert Kubey and Mihaly Csikszentmihalyi, *Television and the Quality of Life* (Hillsdale, New Jersey: Erlbaum Associates, 1990), p. 189.
31. The Morelia Symposium Declaration, "Approaching the Year 2000," reprinted *as an advertisement* in the *New York Times*, November 1, 1991, sec. A, p. 18. The newspaper apparently did not see the Declaration as a newsworthy item and the Symposium had to pay to get the statement into the nation's foremost newspaper.
32. Bernard Weinraub, "Ovitz Firm Gets AT&T Executive," *New York Times*, June 17, 1994, sec. C, p. 1.

5

THE INFORMATION SUPERHIGHWAY: LATEST BLIND ALLEY?

The Information Superhighway: Latest Blind Alley?

American experience with the waves of new communication technology in the twentieth century reveals at least two characteristics present over the decades: one is the overblown promise greeting its appearance; the other is the rapid assumption by corporate custodians of the new instrumentation and processes for commercial ends, i.e., profitmaking. The high expectations for the new means of transmitting messages and images are invariably thwarted by the institutional arrangements that quickly enfold the new instrumentation. This has been the fate, successively, of radio, television, cable, satellite communication, and, still underway, digitized electronic transmission.

In the 1990s the new and advanced information technologies—computers, fiber optics, personal communications products, cyberspace networks—are extolled as "empowering." They are described as the instrumentation that will provide individual autonomy, and, no less important, that they will afford a competitive edge to those who employ them. It is surely a historical irony that as substantive content disappears in much of the media product, a varied range of media technologies are coming on-line (literally), to provide means of producing and transporting a growing volume of new media products to audiences.

The selling of these new information technologies is far more intense today than were the promotions of a half-century ago. This is partly so because the focus, for the moment at least, is domestic. In the 1950s, the sales pitch and enthusiasm for communication technology were directed mainly to the leaders and decision makers—purchasing agents—of less industrialized states. In the United States television didn't need an excessive sales effort. It sold itself. More important, in the 1950s, the American economy commanded the world market. There was no need for new means to achieve world domination. It existed. The concern was to hold back what threatened to be a massive move of numerous countries to some form of nonmarket, socialist-organized economies. Accordingly, the emphasis on information technology as a solvent for social distress was directed, for the most part, outward. Communication technology for development was the recipe for "the other." This no longer describes the global or domestic condition.

Today, crisis is everywhere, especially observable in the United States. As a direct consequence of the *systemic* prioritization of for-profit activities, whereby the public sector is left in a state of squalor and the private affluence of a part of the population exceeds all limits, the American infrastructure, physical and social, is falling apart. Roads, schools, basic utilities and services, and transport are disasters waiting to explode. Two examples will suffice. First, a General Accounting Office (GAO) report to Congress in early 1995 noted that "one third of the nation's 80,000 public schools are in such poor repair that the fourteen million children who attend them are being housed in unsuitable or unsafe conditions."[1] Second, a study of Child Day Care centers, also released at the beginning of 1995, had these findings: "The care provided by most childcare centers is so poor that it threatens children's intellectual and emotional development . . . As many as 40% of infant and toddler rooms provided poor care . . . Overall, 12% of the centers studied were actually unsafe or unsanitary . . . and only one in seven offered the kind of warm relationships that teach children how to trust adults and the intellectual stimulation that helps children become ready for school."[2]

Social statistics reveal a steadily widening gap between the incomes of the well-off and the rest of the population. A census report released in December 1994 showed huge disparities between the incomes of the rich and poor in cities across the country. In New York, for example, the poorest fifth of the population earned an average $5,237 while the richest fifth had an average $110,199. In Los Angeles, the corresponding figures were $6,821 and $123,098.[3] The largest corporations, responding to, or anticipating, international competitive pressure, are busily laying off labor. At the same time, *production does not decline.* Increasingly computerized facilities do nicely with a disappearing work force. To add to the insecurity of American workers, factories and jobs are exported to locales where pay scales are lower and governments offer incentives—generally at the expense of their own working populations.

Alongside the physical and institutional breakdowns, steadily more visible, are rampaging violence and crime that have their origins in a systematic misallocation of resources. Public sector decay and contracting job opportunities hardly provide the soil for community harmony. Only the "entertainment" industry benefits from the rising tide of horror stories that provide the bulk of the daily TV and cable "human interest" programs. This sector, unlike the overall economy, exhibits robust growth. Over a two-year period from 1993 to 1995, the public has had its attention focused, for months on end, on (among other diversions) sensational murder trials, a hired assault on a popular athlete, the castration of a bullying husband, and an especially sordid attack on an innocent victim in an adultery triangle. The televised O.J. Simpson murder trial in 1994 and 1995 became the longest "TV show" in American history.

These "entertainments" unfold at the same time as the country is awash in sordid deals, corrupt officials, general malfeasance, and numerous scandals. Meanwhile, the jails are overflowing, mostly with those from the lower end of the income scale. These prisoners cannot afford the high-priced lawyers the middle and upper-middle classes have access to when in trouble. Their crimes are generally cruder and therefore instantly observable and punishable because their opportunities for sophisticated swindling and bribery are nonexistent. The country's political leadership, unwilling to face root causes, for fear of unpopularity, or, more likely, its concern with the political danger of honestly illuminating social reality, bipartisanly demands a tougher clamp-down on crime. To add to this human drama of misfortune, the homeless in America now total in the millions.[4]

It is in this climate of deepening social distress and willful inattention to its sources that the latest summons for technology to assume the role of all-powerful fixer is issued. From its outset, the Clinton Administration has displayed great faith in the manifold capabilities of new technology, especially information instrumentation and processes. In one of his first speeches as President, Clinton said, "To keep the United States on the cutting edge, my job as President is to adjust America so we can win in the twenty-first century."[5]

Silicon Valley was a site of Clinton's early electioneering in 1992, to which he has returned regularly. Not by accident did John Sculley, then CEO of Apple Computer, sit next to Hillary Rodham Clinton at the President's first appearance before Congress. So too, Vice President Al Gore is repeatedly identified publicly as an informed enthusiast of high-tech information products and processes. His expertise, or at least proficiency, with a computer keyboard receives national television coverage. The new leader of the Republican Party in the House of Representatives, Newt Gingrich, is no less a believer in the capabilities of electronic information to solve the nation's ills.

The Administration's vision of, and reliance on, high-tech communications as the ultimate answer to whatever is ailing the country, was unveiled in September 1993 with the issuance of a governmental task force's report, "National Information Infrastructure (NII): Agenda for Action."[6] Vice President Gore repeated and amplified the report's proposals in a speech at UCLA in early January, 1994.[7] A governmental White Paper, issued at the same time, elaborated further. Hearings were held in 1994 on several bills in Congress that took up these matters. New proposals were being introduced in the 104th Congress. Here, only the general contours of the proposed policies, and their alleged promise, are examined. Details and specifics continue to be formulated; these are almost certain to change over time. The underlying perspectives and assumptions, unfortunately, are likely to endure. It is these that merit scrutiny.

To appreciate the argument that the Government and its congressional bipartisan supporters, to say nothing of the corporate sector, are making for the proposed national information infrastructure, it is instructive, indeed eye-opening, to read at least the introductory section of the September 1993's "Agenda For Action." What follows here, is the text of the document (in italics), interspersed with my interrogation of the claims.

The Promise of the NII

Imagine you had a device that combined a telephone, a TV, a camcorder, and a personal computer. No matter where you went or what time it was, your child could see you and talk to you, you could watch a replay of your team's last game, you could browse the latest editions to the library, or you could find the best prices in town on groceries, furniture, clothes—whatever you needed.

Imagine having to be in twenty-four-hour, uninterrupted contact with your children. Some would regard this as a description of hell. As for watching a replay of your team's last game, in most instances, this event would be best forgotten. The vista of library riches at everyone's immediate disposal overlooks the possible shutdown and elimination of public libraries; the shopping prospects are really what the new instrumentation is all about.

Imagine further the dramatic changes in your life if:

The best schools, teachers, and courses were available to all students, without regard to geography, distance, resources, or disability.

What happens to the rest of the schools? Are they to be shuttered and the kids put on line exclusively to Harvard, Yale, and a few posh private high schools? Who needs a school *system* if attention is focused and channeled on a few select centers of supposed excellence? More worrisome still, there is the implicit trust that technology can substitute for human interactions in the learning process. In assessing the character of a newly-appointed Secretary of Defense, in February 1994, one observer wrote: "he's [William J. Perry] identified with a technocratic position and believes in using technology to substitute for humans on the battlefield."[8] This may be a splendid means for reducing war casualties, but is it transferable to education? It is still too early to make a full assessment of the electronic classroom, but first reports are less than reassuring.

A pioneer cyberspace university, Phoenix University in San Francisco, was the subject of a *Wall Street Journal* report. One thousand of its eighteen thousand students are earning their degrees via computer. The school "has no fraternities, dormitories, or football team . . . [it] *doesn't even have a library,* just a research desk with a toll-free telephone number. Perhaps more to the point, " . . . none of Phoenix's 2,100 instructors are tenured or full-time. They are independent contractors paid about $1,000 to $1,200 per course." This is the equivalent of the minimum wage in industry.[9]

Replacement part-time classroom teachers, hooked up to distant students by cable and fiber optics, however extolled as an educational advance, is better seen as yet another sign of technological subterfuge, seeking to mask the decay in the nation's public schooling. To hail it as a benefit is, wittingly or not, gross deception.

The vast resources of art, literature, and science were available everywhere, not just in large institutions or big city libraries and museums.

This is well and good. But what will motivate the kids to dip into these treasures if the bulk of their social environment is filled with the more commercially favored activities of shopping, inane entertainment, and grisly sensationalism?

Services that improve America's health care system and respond to other important social needs were available on-line, without waiting in line, when and where you needed them.

Before providing on-line health care, the health system itself has to be rescued from its current administrators—the insurance, hospital, drug and privileged medical interests. This is a *social,* not a technological, issue. Yet apart from the basic institutional question, the on-line health care scenario that Washington suggests is another instance of substituting a technology for human hands-on care. To anyone who has tried to reach the major welfare bureaucracies—Social Security, for example—by telephone, the promise of "not waiting in line," is fanciful, at best. For many years Americans have been conditioned to believe that house calls by physicians are evidence of "underdevelopment." Increased, probably near-exclusive, distance-diagnosis seems the chosen path of the information highway proponents. Is this a demonstrated benefit, or is it a justification of an unwillingness to attend to people's needs in a human fashion?

You could live in many places without forgoing opportunities for useful and fulfilling employment, by "telecommuting" to your office through an electronic highway instead of by automobile, bus or train.

Reducing commuting time and the energy expenditure connected with it are certainly desirable. Yet these goals is achievable in other ways, e.g., mass transit or planned business location. Telecommuting as a way of national life moves people further along the course to an atomized, community-destroying existence. Even now it characterizes much of American life. Is more of this deliberately sought?

Small manufacturers could get orders from all over the world electronically—with detailed specifications—in a form that the machines could use to produce the necessary items.

It is thoughtful of Washington to consider the needs of smaller businesses. Perhaps those needs would be better served if national policy enforced the antitrust laws and, thereby, allowed smaller enterprises some breathing space from the giant outfits that are concentrating resources—more about this below—at a frenzied pace.

You could see the latest movies, play the hottest video games, or bank and shop from the comfort of your home whenever you chose.

This is the meat and potatoes of the national information highway as it is currently viewed by corporate America. The circuitry's capability to carry the product of the communications-cultural conglomerates into the nation's living rooms is what has the corporate communications sector salivating. This, and the marketers' dream to come into the home and rouse the residents to active home shopping are the mainsprings of the plan's motivation. Telephone companies, computer firms, cable systems, and entertainment conglomerates are rushing to build the links that will funnel this commercial flow into home television sets and/or computer terminals.

You could obtain government information directly or through local organizations like libraries, apply for and receive government benefits electronically, and get in touch with government officials easily.

This could occur, and if it does, it will be a healthy development. Yet here, too, the intervening institutional roadblocks are considerable. Will the increasingly influential commercial information sector accept a larger role for public institutions? In recent years, developments have been mostly in the other direction—the enhancement of the private information provider at the expense of the public one. The commercialization of information and the ever-growing concentration of information producers are dominant features of the present American economy. As for getting in touch easily with government officials, the same caution expressed about long-distance medical assistance is warranted.

Individual government agencies, businesses and other entities all could exchange information electronically—reducing paperwork and improving services.

The emphasis on "reducing paperwork" dates back to the Reagan years, when far-reaching measures to eliminate thousands of government documents and reports were justified by claiming it represented a reduction of paperwork. It was actually an assault on many socially valuable public activities, and was in keeping with that Administration's, and the succeeding one's, deliberate policy to reduce the public sector in American life. Perhaps the reassertion of this objective now signifies efforts toward conservation. It is always perilous to adopt the language of an adversary doctrine and policy; there are other dangers as well. In the waning days of the Bush Administration, for example, frantic efforts were made to electronically "shred" executive documents; that is, to dispose of computer tapes. In the first weeks of the Clinton regime there was what can only be described as collusion in this activity. (See chapter 3.)

In sum, the "imaginings" of the Task Force on The National Information Infrastructure and allied enthusiasts about the promise of the electronic highway raise more doubts than hopes. When the basic assumptions that underlie the "promise" of the new technological enterprise are taken into account, there is little room for hopeful imaginings.

All Power to the Corporate Sector

Eighty or so years ago, in another setting, Lenin issued a revolutionary policy, proclaiming "All Power to the Soviets." Metaphorically, Washington has taken up the call, but with a slightly different emphasis. The Clinton-Gore leadership, with full bipartisan support in Congress, is calling for all power to the corporate communication sector. The "Agenda for Action" document sounds this cry loudly and repeatedly. Following the already-cited prospectus of extravagant expectations for the National Information Infrastructure, comes this message:

> The private sector will lead the deployment of the NII. In recent years, U.S. companies have invested more than $50 billion annually in telecommunications infrastructure . . . businesses [are] responsible for creating and operating the NII.[10]

In his speech in Los Angeles, Vice President Gore reiterated:

> We begin with two of our basic principles—the need for private investment and fair competition. The nation needs private investment to complete the construction of the National Information Infrastructure. And competition is the single most critical means of encouraging that private investment.[11]

Private ownership and competition in the use of the electronic information highway are Washington's basic prescriptions for the infrastructure that promises to carry, for business and home use, all the image and message and data flow that the country produces. When the September 1993 Agenda was issued, the overnight response of the American Library Association pointedly focused on the ownership question. It queried:

> While admitting that the federal government has a key leadership role to play
> in NII development, the Administration assumes that "the private sector will
> build and run virtually all of the National Information Infrastructure." *Yet this
> is the emerging infrastructure for communications—the activity that makes us
> human. The stakes for a democratic society are high, and market forces alone
> will not ensure that societal goals are met.*[12]

The ALA's assessment of the inadequacy of market forces in providing social needs has been demonstrated across five centuries of global, and two
centuries of American capitalist development. Whatever social improvements have occurred (e.g., shorter working day, Social Security, elimination
of child labor) have come mostly from social struggle. Market forces systematically ignored—where they did not combat—the needs of the majority. The current enthusiasm for market forces, hardly a popular
phenomenon, is no long-standing affair.

Relatedly, and reflecting the postwar increase in conservative influence
in America, much has been written about whether ownership really matters.
According to this thinking, which also has a very brief history, it is of no
consequence if an enterprise is privately or governmentally owned. It will
still be subject to the same economic forces and these will produce near-
identical results regardless of the ownership factor. It follows—according
to this logic—that social custodianship is pointless. Yet this is by no means
self-evident. If it were the case, why the unyielding insistence, in recent
decades, on the necessity for privatization? Also, why should private investors and corporations, be stampeding to spend an estimated $500 billion
to build the information infrastructure if it didn't matter who owned it?

The answer is *it does matter.* Those who put up the capital make the basic
decisions. Some of these, in the time ahead, will be: who will build the highway and where will it be built; who will be admitted to the highway; what
will be the conditions of that admission; what will flow over the highway and
in what volume; who will take care of monitoring the communications that,
in the words of the American Library Association, "make us human"?

Washington offers assurances on all these matters. It is competition, it insists, that will assure the common good. The Administration places its main
reliance on competition to keep prices down, to thwart the emergence of
monopoly, to stimulate investment, to provide new jobs, to increase exports,
to harmonize government-business-labor relations, and, probably, to eliminate the common cold. "Today," Vice President Gore explains, "we must
choose competition again and protect it against both suffocating regulation
on the one hand and unfettered monopolies on the other . . . the pressure of
competition will be great—and it will drive continuing advancements in
technology, quality and cost . . . . we expect open competition to bring lower
prices and better services . . ."[13]

It demonstrates great faith to look forward to the beneficent workings of competition in the 1990s when the concentration of American capital has reached awesome levels. Having just completed a decade of spectacular mergers, consolidations, take-overs, leveraged buy-outs, and frenzied concentration of assets, corporate America knows, and tolerates, little restraint.

This was the message publicly flaunted in October 1993, when the Bell Atlantic Corporation and Tele-Communications, Inc. announced their intention to merge. "It was the biggest merger ever in the communications industry, giving birth to a behemoth that will reach twenty-three per cent of American homes, will be able to call upon sixty billion dollars in assets, and will rank as the sixth-largest American company." [14] That this merger was not consummated was no indication that monopoly power was being checked. It fell apart because it was unacceptable to Atlantic Bell's main shareholders—who sought more favorable terms.

The proposed union was not a lone event. Across the United States economy and especially in the communications sector concentration of companies and assets are being made at a frenetic pace. In what is described as "a frenzy of deal-making," cable, telephone, and computer software companies are uniting, and are moving to swallow entertainment and broadcasting properties. [15] Entertainment conglomerates like Time Warner and Disney have other ideas about their fate. There is no need, nor is it possible, to specify the specific outcomes of these corporate maneuvers. What *is* essential is to recognize that this massive communications merger movement provides the context, and the motivation, for the national information infrastructure project. Indeed, Vice President Gore acknowledges this:

> [The] . . . communication industries are moving to the unified information market-place of the future. [To meet this development,] . . . we must move from the traditional adversarial relationship between business and government to a more productive relationship based on consensus. We must build a new model of public-private cooperation . . . [16]

This should not prove too difficult as long as Washington continues to satisfy business' agenda. This it is doing with enthusiasm. In September 1993, for example, the government delivered an inestimably precious gift of a vital natural resource to private interests: it announced its intention to sell a chunk of the radio spectrum—the resource that enables broadcasting and numerous other communication capabilities to be realized. The proposal was couched in the familiar upbeat, "we will all benefit from this" language. Government spokespeople emphasized that the public would receive many billions of dollars from the sale. An additional public benefit, it was affirmed, claimed that the management of the spectrum would be "improved." "Market principles" would see to that. [17]

In short, the disposition of a portion of a major national *and* natural resource has gone to corporate business. This action overturns a long-standing principle of protecting the spectrum from a sell-off to private interests. However inadequate the management has been in the twentieth century— half of the spectrum in the hands of the military and some of it on lease to broadcasters and other private users—the resource until now, *always has been accountable*, at least in principle, to public authority. No longer! A chunk of the spectrum has been sold to private communications colossi, the super companies that have been created in recent years. And here again, the policy is not what it appears to be.

Perhaps to reduce the possible outcry over selling off a public property to giant communications enterprises, the Federal Communications Commission established a policy of "set-asides," that is, insisting that some of the spectrum go to small businesses and minority interests. However, the rules for the auction made it likely that the big companies would not be shut out of these reserved frequencies either. The Commission allowed the big corporate investors to acquire "75% of the equity and 49.9% of the voting stock" of the companies receiving the set-asides.[18] This is tantamount to a full negation of the "affirmative action" provisions, which are increasingly under attack from almost all quarters. Given the huge costs of starting a communication business, few small entrepreneurs will be able to go it alone. Of necessity, they will be obliged to call upon the capital of the big investors. And with a rich historical experience to draw upon, it is safe to say that the newcomers will soon be dispossessed of their shares.

In fact, the sale, completed in March 1995, did bring billions into the public treasury. Not surprisingly, it also turned over to a handful of telecommunications/cable giants most of the auctioned spectrum space. AT&T, the regional Bell companies, Sprint, and Telecommunications, Inc., were the main winners. "This auction," the *New York Times'* telecommunications reporter observed, "was for big players only."[19]

However impressive the proceeds of the sale, what is not mentioned is that the spectrum is a renewable resource—one that never is exhausted or depleted by its use. Its sale is a *one-time* payment for owning and deriving profit from a resource that may go on into perpetuity. A dubious bargain for the public! But beyond the spectrum's revenue-producing capability, there is another vital public interest at stake in its sale: it puts private commercial interests in charge of *the contents* of a slice of a basic natural resource. Alternatively, social utilization is precluded for as long as this property transfer is allowed to stand.

While the government exuberantly ratifies the private construction of the national information infrastructure, it claims it will not ignore the needs of the public. Universal service will be maintained and information differentials among the population will not be tolerated, it says. Perhaps. But the mechanism (competition) that will secure these social goals is faulty, and the guardians who will oversee the process are weak and puny in comparison with the power clusters they are supposed to oversee. (The concept of regulation as a legitimate function of government has practically disappeared.)

The regulatory agencies, rarely bulldogs of vigilance in the past, are today, with few exceptions, close to being corporate auxiliaries. This condition has evolved because the institutional power of business has grown to far exceed that of government, to say nothing of the general public. This was not always the situation, at least not to the same extent. In fact, the creation of most of the oversight agencies came about from strong social movements that protested the exploitative and discriminatory behavior of the railroads, the banks, the telegraph and the telephone monopolies, the food processors, and the security markets in the nineteenth and early twentieth centuries.[20] Today, such movements either are absent or feeble. Their presence would be the only true public safeguard in the current corporate-driven rush to construct an information structure according to its own design and interests. In any case, the protection of the public's interest in the information infrastructure, now being built, is assigned, in the main, to competition—the rivalries of billion-dollar communication companies—and, to administrative agencies presently unequal, either through structural weakness or disinclination, to the job.

Vice President Gore states that "The responsibility to design specific measures to achieve these aims [universal service and the avoidance of the creation of a class of "information haves" and another of "have nots"] will be delegated to the Federal Communications Commission."[21] This is the Agency that has presided with serenity over the vast integration and concentration of resources in the communications industry in the last twenty years. To paraphrase Will Rogers, an icon of another time, the FCC rarely met a merger it didn't like, or an expansion of industry/company power it didn't approve. Paradoxically, it is the government's unqualified reliance on competition between phone, cable, computer, and entertainment companies and industries to provide universal service at low prices that almost inevitably will further extend and deepen the cultural-informational crisis that even now tears apart the national social fabric.

There has been no lack of *a certain kind* of competition between the dominant three, now four, national broadcasting networks. ABC, CBS, NBC, and Fox are at each other's throats, striving, with ever more degraded shows, for audience-viewing rating points. This, in large part, is the explanation for the unidimensionality of the programming across all the networks, and independents as well. It accounts also for the exclusion of critical material and the media's general preoccupation, if not obsession, with a daily menu of sensational and ugly events.

Responding, for example, to public criticism over one especially offensive program, *The Jerry Springer Show,* the president of NBC, a subsidiary of $60 billion General Electric, said the time when the show is aired "is not my best moment of the day." In the next breath he added: "It's obvious the audience is out there."[22] And that's the clinching factor. It is notable also, that the companies that own or sponsor and screen these shows are not fringe enterprises. Time Warner, NBC, Sears, and Procter & Gamble constitute the central core of U.S. media-cultural activity.

Competition and market forces are already at work in anticipation of the expanded capabilities of the system-in-construction. One prospect is "a string of cable 'marketing channels,' each dedicated to the selling of one category of big-ticket consumer products." This is not to be confused with home shopping channels, e.g., QVC, and others, now in full and successful operation. If the private "planners" have their way, one channel will be reserved exclusively, each for the display and sale of automobiles, or washing machines, or yachts or sofas.[23] Other likely candidates for the expanded channel capacity are the Crime Channel, the Game Channel, the Golf Channel, the Military Channel, the Television Food Network, and lots more. A *Financial Times* report offered an especially imaginative use of the interactive services in the offing:

> ... technology could further extend the market by offering gambling opportunities through the electronic super-highway now beginning to evolve—in other words, allowing people to gamble in their homes by taking part in interactive casino games using cable channels and their television screens.[24]

None of these appalling prospects is a future certainty. They are the early warning markers of what is in store *if* the market is left to its own designs. There is certainly enough historical experience to draw on and, one would hope, to learn from. Radio, for example, as did television, initially offered enormous potential for the public's health and social benefit. This has been squandered by the tide of commercialism that has engulfed both media. This is the pattern now being extended to the electronic age.

The safeguards promised by Washington, and accepted by most of the public interest groups in the field, to allay the crassest effects of market and competitive arrangements on the information infrastructure, seem to overlook one central and decisive question: How can the national information/entertainment/cultural product include genuine diversity? This is a question separate from universality and ability to pay for service, both of which are obviously of great importance. But the *contents* of the information flow is the ultimate and overriding issue.

This is not to be confused with the spurious and insistent media and carrier owners' boast of supplying the public with "choice." It is not a matter of selecting from six crime dramas, or sitcoms, or innumerable special effects-filled movies. Neither is it the capability to select one or another carrier systems or electronic delivery products. Diversity is achieved when the *full spectrum* of American talent and creativity is enlisted, *and supported,* by *public revenues.* These are the sole guarantees of meaningful choice. Has anyone at an authoritative level, for example, suggested that at least *half* of the alleged forthcoming five hundred channels be allocated to public use, along with the resources to make the allocation implementable? Regrettably, even the public interest groups seem resigned, if not satisfied, to accept residual concessions from the governmental-corporate alliance.

The gap between good intentions and practical outcomes, and the contradiction between social benefit and private interest, is especially notable in the government's formula for utilizing the new electronic technologies. Inquiring about the direction of the telecommunications developments underway, Ken Auletta, in the *New Yorker,* made this observation: "The Clinton Administration wants the superhighway to have public channels, but it doesn't want to expend public dollars to accomplish that; it wants rigorous enforcement of the antitrust laws, yet also wants friendly relations with corporate America. Sometimes, obviously, such goals collide."[25]

One more time in American history, a new communications technology is being promoted with uncritical acclaim, while it is being turned over to corporate management. Cautionary voices, and there are a few, point out the folly of the current policy. George Brown, for example, the former chairman of the House Committee on Science, Space, and Technology, insists that "Our most serious problems are social problems for which there are no technical solutions, only human solutions."[26] So, too, Les Brown, veteran TV critic and observer, playfully notes "The Seven Deadly Sins of the Digital Age," which he sees as: "1. Inequality; 2. Commercial exploitation and information abuse; 3. Threats to personal privacy; 4. The disintegration of community; 5. Instant plebiscites and the distortion of democracy; 6. The tyranny of gatekeepers, and 7. The loss of public service values and social responsibility."[27] These warnings remain unacceptable to dominant thinking and there is no reason, therefore, to believe that the information highway outcome will be more satisfactory than media technology uses have been throughout the twentieth century.

Yet there is one critical difference today that raises the stakes considerably: Digital technology reduces *all* images and messages to common bits that can be transmitted through the new circuitry. To take advantage of this, the separate industrial sectors that formerly either transmitted or produced messages and images are uniting into a tiny number of rich and powerful companies. Increasingly, these will produce and disseminate the country's *total* cultural substance. This foretells a time when most of the ingredients of national consciousness, failing serious effort to defend the common good, will be completely under the control of a handful of private, giant, communications conglomerates.

In France, where the national cultural condition is taken seriously, a former and now discredited Minister of Communications worried about the direction and impact on France, and elsewhere, of these American developments. Concerned with American TV programs and movies being beamed down from satellites, he called the instrumentation "a genuine war machine." Paraphrasing Vice President Gore, but from a strikingly different perspective, he wrote, "audiovisual is the major strategic prize of the next century and the European market the principal target of the big American communications groups."[28] French concerns are justified, but there is a misapprehension. The first "principal target" is the U. S. domestic population—us! After the home front has been saturated, others sites, the French not excluded, will receive proper attention.

Notes

1. William H. Honan, "Many U.S Schools Are Unsafe," *New York Times*, February 2, 1995, sec. A, p. 7.
2. Susan Chira, "Care at Child Day Centers Is Rated Poor," *New York Times*, February 7, 1995, sec. A, p. 6.
3. Sam Roberts, "Gap Between Rich and Poor in New York Grows Wider," *New York Times*, December 26, 1994, p. 20.
4. Jason De Parle, "Report to Clinton Sees Vast Extent of Homelessness," *New York Times*, February 17, 1994, p. 1.
5. John Markoff, "Clinton Proposes Changes in Policy to Aid Technology," New York Times, February 23, 1993, p. 1.
6. The National Information Infrastructure: The Administration's Agenda for Action, Washington, D.C., September 15, 1993.
7. Remarks by Vice President Al Gore, Royce Hall, UCLA, Los Angeles, California, January 11, 1994. Hereafter cited as "Gore speech."
8. John Markoff, "New Defense Dept. Chief Put High Tech in Arms, *New York Times*, February 5, 1994, p. 9.
9. Steve Stecklow, "At Phoenix University Class Can Be Anywhere—Even in Cyberspace," *Wall Street Journal*, September 12, 1994, p. 1. Emphasis added.
10. Agenda for Action, op cit.
11. Gore speech.
12. ALAWON, American Library Association, Washington Office, Vol. 2, No. 38 (September 16, 1993). Italics added.
13. Gore speech.
14. Ken Auletta, "John Malone: Flying Solo," *New Yorker*, February 7, 1994, p. 52.
15. Edmund L. Andrews, "Sweeping Revision in Communication Is on the Horizon," *New York Times*, October 3, 1994, p. 1.
16. Gore speech.

17. Agenda for Action, op cit.
18. Edmund L. Andrews, "U.S. Seeks Military Airwaves to Make Way for Private Use," *New York Times*, February 10, 1994, p. 1., and, Edmund L. Andrews, "F.C.C. Approves Set-Asides for Its Wireless Auctions," *New York Times*, June 30, 1994.
19. Edmund L. Andrews, "Winners of Wireless Auction to Pay $7 Billion," *New York Times*, March 14, 1995, sec. C, p. 1.
20. Robert W. McChesney, *Telecommunications, Mass Media and Democracy* (New York: Oxford University Press, 1993). See also Dan Schiller, "'Everybody's Common Means of Communications'? The Origins of the Public Service Conception in U.S. Telecommunications 1894–1919," paper presented at the Organization of American Historians Annual Meeting, Atlanta, April 14–17, 1994.
21. Gore speech.
22. Bill Carter, "After Killing, Hard Questions for Talk Shows," *New York Times*, March 14, 1995, p. 1.
23. "A Shopping Channel for All," *Broadcasting and Cable*, October 25, 1993, p. 25.
24. Richard Tomkins, "Rush to Place their Bets," *Financial Times*, January 16, 1994, p. 7.
25. Ken Auletta, "Under the Wire," *New Yorker*, January 17, 1994, p. 52.
26. George E. Brown, Jr., quoted in the *Chronicle of Higher Education*, June 1, 1994, sec. B, p. 5.
27. Les Brown, "The Seven Deadly Sins of the Digital Age," *Intermedia*, Vol. 22, No. 3, (July 1994), pp. 32–37.
28. Richard W. Stevenson, "Lights! Camera! Europe!" *New York Times*, February 6, 1994, sec. 3, p. 1.

6

GLOBALIZING THE ELECTRONIC HIGHWAY: CREATING AN UNGOVERNABLE WORLD

Globalizing the Electronic Highway: Creating an Ungovernable World

While plans abound and steps are taken to construct the electronic information highway as rapidly as possible *inside* the continental boundaries, the design for a global system is hardly overlooked. In March 1994, Vice President Al Gore traveled to Buenos Aires, the site of an International Telecommunications Union Conference, at which representatives from 132 countries were present. There, Gore repeated, before an international audience, the great promise he saw in electronic communication. He extended his vision to a global setting:

> . . . we now have at hand the technological breakthroughs and economic means to bring all the communities in the world together. We now can at last create a planetary information network that transmits messages and images with the speed of light from the largest city to the smallest village on every continent.

After offering this transcendental vision Gore concluded, more pragmatically, that this information network "will be a means by which families and friends will transcend the barriers of time and distance . . . and it will make possible a global information marketplace, where consumers can buy and sell products." Buying and selling information goods on the global network, no less than on the domestic one, Gore insisted, required that private industry be in charge. "We propose that private investment and competition be the foundations for development of the GII [Global Information Infrastructure]."[1]

Months earlier a somewhat different emphasis was given to the electronic communication project, perhaps understandably, in a domestic venue. In September 1993, the White House described the electronic highway as a means "to enable U.S. firms to compete and win in the global economy," and to give the domestic economy a "competitive edge" internationally.[2] Not mentioned (out of graciousness?) in Buenos Aires, but clearly in the forefront of White House thinking, is the global command and direction of the world economy through information control, and the subsequent benefits. Such a goal expressed for the first time by a new administration is nothing new. For more than half a century, beginning during World War II, U.S. leadership recognized the centrality of information control for gaining world advantage. Well before most of the world could do much about it, U.S. groups, private and governmental, were actively promoting information and cultural primacy on all continents. The policy had many elements, not all of them necessarily deliberate.

In the 1990s, for example, with a new generation of leadership coming into authority around the world, it is a familiar phenomenon to discover that this or that individual, taking over the reins in this or that country, has been educated in the United States. By no means unique in this respect, Mexico provides a striking case in point; its departing president is a Harvard graduate, its newly designated leader is from Yale. This situation exists in many places. The education and training of foreign students in American schools and universities, expanded greatly after World War II, are now producing their harvest of graduates who assume high office at home. They have imbibed of free market and other doctrines and values ladled out in America's premier schools.

But U.S. global cultural influence has not been limited to formal education. U.S. films and TV programs are the chief fare of national systems in most countries. News programs, especially CNN, offer U.S. perspectives, sometimes the *only* perspective provided, to world audiences. American recorded music, theme parks (Disney et al.) and advertising now comprise a good part of the world's cultural environment. No less phenomenal is the ad hoc adoption of English as the world's second language. Facilitating this development have been the waves of U.S. pop culture that have washed across all frontiers for forty years. Once the preeminence of English has been established, Anglo-U.S. ideas, values, and cultural products generally are received with familiarity and enthusiasm in the global arena.

All this is well known and amply documented, though the domestic media and political establishments are remarkably shy in acknowledging their de facto cultural domination of what they like to refer to as "the global market." What is of special interest here, however, is the skillful combination that fuses information instrumentation and philosophic principle. It is this mix that fuels the push toward concentrated cultural power. The development has not been a chance occurrence. Strategic planning, rarely identified as such, has been present throughout. And it has succeeded well beyond the initial expectations of its formulators.

At the outset of what some hoped would be an American Century, a vital doctrine was promoted: the free flow of information.[3] This principle, when considered out of context, seems unexceptional, and indeed, entitled to respect. Yet when viewed alongside the reality of the early postwar years, it conferred unmatchable advantage on the U.S. cultural industries. No rival foreign film industry, TV production center, publishing enterprise, or news establishment could possibly have competed on equal terms with the powerful U.S. media-entertainment companies at that time. And so it has gone to this day. The free flow of information, in its implementation, has meant the ascendance of U.S. cultural products worldwide.

Along with the free-flow principle U.S. global strategy supported the rapid and fullest development of transport and information technologies, both of which underpinned the capability for the cultural domination that was being constructed. To this day, although less than in previous years, most of the civilian airliners in operation in most countries are made in America. These are also the vehicles that have allowed the massive growth of the world tourist industry, which has, in turn, leaned heavily on U.S. modes of entertaining and nurturing tourists, i.e., chain hotels, packaged tours, constructed spectacles, and so on. These developments were commercially-driven, but their consequences were no less cultural.

Two key sectors received special attention, and unstinting resources from the U.S. Government, in the never-ending pursuit of winning and holding the global market for U.S. products and services. Satellite communications, which radically improved telecommunications, and removed distance as a factor in global production, and computerization, which has become the basis of the information-using economy, have long been the recipients of heavy subsidies and favored treatment, Washington's enthusiastic rhetoric for "free markets," notwithstanding.

Present plans to construct an electronic information highway closely follow the U.S. effort in the development and deployment of the communication satellite. The satellite project had one unambiguous goal. It was intended, and succeeded, in capturing control of international communication circuits from British cable interests. The imperial rule of Great Britain in the nineteenth and early twentieth centuries had been facilitated greatly by control of the underwater message flow between the colonies and London. The American-built and controlled satellite bypassed the cable and helped to break the Empire's monopoly on trade and investment, and to reduce the British role in international communication.[4]

Control of information instrumentation, invariably, goes hand in hand with control of the message flow, its content, surveillance capability, and all forms of information intelligence. To be sure, the revenues from such control are hardly afterthoughts. Building and owning the electronic information highway will confer similar advantages, as did the earlier cables, to their monopolizers. Yet once again the alleged promise of the communications instrumentation, represented by the GII (global information infrastructure), stresses the general social benefit. However, the conditions attached to the proposal—private creation and ownership of the global highway—make it inevitable that the network, when built, will be of most value to those who currently have the financial ability to satisfy their need for instantaneous and voluminous global message flows. (These "users," let it be recalled, are transnational companies that constitute the driving force for the creation of a global marketplace, deregulated world arena, and global production sites selected for profitability and convenience. As might be expected, these are also the central considerations behind both worldwide and domestic electronic highway projects.)

The launching of the global information highway project comes at a time when most, if not all, of the preconditions for a corporate global "order" are in place. There is, first the actual existence of a global economy, organized and directed by a relatively tiny number of global (transnational) corporations. According to a survey of this global economic apparatus, 37,000 companies currently make up the system. As there are millions of businesses in the United States—let alone those in Germany, Japan, and elsewhere—the extent of the concentration of economic influence in this global system can not be overstated. It exceeds our experience to comprehend it. And though 37,000 companies currently occupy the command posts of the world economic order, the largest 100 transnational companies, in 1990, "had about $3.2 trillion in global assets of which $1.2 trillion was outside their own home countries."[5]

These few hundred megafirms are the true power wielders of this era. This world corporate order, and its concentrated core in particular, has been a major force in greatly reducing the influence of nation states. As private economic decisions increasingly govern, among other functions, the global and national allocation of resources, the amount and character of investment, the value of currencies, and the sites and modes of production—many of the important duties of government—have been appropriated, silently for the most part, by these giant private economic aggregates.[6] These corporations have been the leading force in promoting deregulation and privatization of industry, in all countries, notably but not exclusively, in the telecommunications sector. *Business Week* in a 1994 report, notes:

> From Italy to Taiwan, scores of governments, caught up in a free market frenzy and needing cash, are selling shares of state-run companies to the public. This sweeping global privatization movement, involving more than fifty nations and expected to raise some $300 billion over five years . . .[7]

This is but one wave of many that have rolled across the international scene in recent years.

The net effect of the large-scale deregulation of industry and the massive privatizations that have occurred, among other consequences, is the increasing inability of national authority to be effective. Unaccountability of the transnational corporation is now the prevailing condition in most countries. With fewer and fewer exceptions the world-active company, on basic decisions that affect huge numbers of people, reports to no one except its own executives and its major shareholders. At the same time, the strength of the transnational sector continues to grow and the companies comprising it are themselves engaged in uninterrupted expansion and concentration.

These developments are especially observable in the communication-media sphere which, naturally, is also the site of the strongest electronic information highway sentiments. As U.S. media and cultural product flow more heavily into the global market, the interests of this sector become increasingly congruent with general transnational corporate objectives and policies. While nonmedia companies—oil, heavy equipment, aerospace, agri-business—seek ever-improved means of communication to carry on and extend their international operations, the media-communication sector is only too happy to make these facilities available, at a price, to be sure. At the same time it strives, generally very successfully, to expand markets for its own specific outputs.

The recent rush to integration in the media-communication sector is itself a remarkable development. What can only be described as *total communication* capability—sometimes called "one-stop communication"—has become a short-term goal of the major firms in this sector. This translates into giant companies that possess the hardware and software to fully control messages and images, from the conceptual stage to their ultimate delivery to users and audiences. In brief, what is intended, and what already is underway, is the creation of private domains that will produce data and entertainment (films, interactive TV programs and video games, recordings, news), package them, transmit them through satellite, cable and/or telephone lines into the living rooms and offices of individuals and businesses.

Which companies ultimately will dominate the world and domestic markets is still uncertain. Time Warner, Viacom, Hearst, Bell Atlantic, Sega, U.S. West, Microsoft, AT&T, IBM, Comcast, and Tele-Communications, Inc., are a few of the big players who are experimenting with and testing , different systems of "full service" communication and vying with each other for advantageous market position.[8] "The long-term economic opportunities" of these activities, Ken Auletta, writing in the *New Yorker*, points out, "excite the business imagination, for the rewards can be stupendous." The sums involved warrant this excitement.

The cable and telephone businesses today [1994] generate close to two hundred billion dollars a year in revenues. Shopping by catalogue and other forms of shopping at home now constitute an eighty-billion-annual business. Entertainment-video stores, movie theatres, theme parks, music, books, video games, theatre, gambling—is a three-hundred-and-forty-billion-dollar business, and is growing twice as fast as over-all consumer spending.[9]

This is the *domestic* market! And it grows rapidly from year to year. The dimensions of the global market are still to be discovered. In any event, corporate communication-entertainment titans are readying their capabilities to fill the cultural space of hundreds of millions of existing and potential users and viewers, at home and abroad. More disturbing still, these global enterprises hope to enjoy and possibly extend their relative immunity to oversight, locally and internationally.

The electronic information highway is being promoted as a powerful means to even out the disparities and inequalities that afflict people inside the United States and throughout the world economy. Vice President Gore's and President Clinton's many statements about the information highway, reassure that the project will reduce the gulf that separates the "haves" from the "have nots" in education, health, and income. Yet the ground condition, the nonnegotiable policy of the project, contradicts that promise.

A privately constructed and owned electronic information system, of necessity, will embody the fundamental features of a private enterprise economy: inequality of income along with the production of goods and services for profit. As production and sales are inseparably connected to income, the overall economy is directed, by the logic of market forces, to producing for, and seeking, those with the most income. This is not illogical, given the features of the system, because this offers the greatest possibility of profit. It follows that a privately owned and managed information highway will be turned toward the interests, needs, and income of the most advantaged sectors of the society. Sometimes this systemic tendency can be modified, but to do so requires the pressure of a strong political movement.

The world as it now exists, with very few (and disappearing?) exceptions, has as one of its central characteristics, income inequality. Much of this inequality has historical roots, but a good part of it also is the direct outcome of the operating effects of privately owned economies worldwide. The most developed countries exhibit wide income inequalities, and the United States is no exception. In the U.S., those at the top income levels—a tiny percentage of the population—are paid more than the total amount earned by half of the nation's workers. In less industrialized countries, most of them still in some sort of economic dependency, the differentials are wider still. In India, for example, 120 million people now enjoy middle-class incomes but 70% of the country's population remain mired in poverty.[10] In Colombia a recent report noted:

The number of people living below the poverty line has increased by about one million since 1990, to include about half of Colombia's population of thirty-three million people. In fifteen years, the gap between average rural and urban incomes doubled.[11]

This widening gap occurred in a period of "growth."

In 1994 a Human Development report of the United Nation's Development Program, wide income gaps between sections of a nation's population are seen as widespread conditions around the world and threaten to lead to chaos in the afflicted areas. Egypt, South Africa, Nigeria, and Brazil, among others, "are countries now in danger of joining the world's list of failed states."[12]

A similar condition of growth alongside immiseration is found in the United States. "Today," writes an economic reporter for the *New York Times*, "the economy can keep on growing with the wealthiest 40% of the nation's families getting 68% of the income, even though 60% of the population is unhappily on the sidelines."[13] Similar conditions exist throughout Latin America, Asia, and Eastern Europe, including Russia. These are all regions of "growth," of this peculiar market variety.

Will the creation of privately financed and owned high-speed, multi-capability circuits carrying broad streams of messages and images, lessen the gaps in living conditions that presently exist across the globe? Time-Warner, AT&T, Microsoft, and their rivals can not be preoccupied with social inequality. Their focus is on revenue. Profits can come only from those who already have the income to purchase the services that are being prepared for sale. In sum, the world of today, the transnationals' world, is, if not *by design*, then certainly by structural character, a divided place, where some prosper and many more languish at the edge. A market-driven industry or economy, national or global, if it is to survive, must cater to the ability-to-pay folks. It may sympathize with, but it cannot give priority to, poorer and marginal strata.

Failing major political interventions—hardly to be expected in a time of worldwide deregulation and political conservatism—income gaps will widen, not diminish, at home and around the world. The inevitable corollary, in communication, is the employment of the electronic circuitry for transnational corporate marketing, internal company operations, and businesses' ideological objectives. Corporate data, Hollywood films and TV programs, business statistics, home gambling, video games, virtual reality shows, and shopping channels are the likely fare on the new electronic circuitry. Welcome to the new world market forces' order!

Yet there is (at least) one cloud moving across this otherwise sunny market forces sky. *How will this corporately organized world be governed?* If national authority continues to decline, and corporate resource allocation and general decision making continue to grow, and the needs and welfare of approximately two-thirds of the world's population go unattended and even deteriorate, what will keep these conditions from provoking large-scale political convulsions in one place after another? And, from the standpoint of the globally privileged, wherever their location, can they be insulated from these inevitable upheavals? What authority, if any, now exists to intervene and check these powerful currents?

These are not matters that come up regularly on the nation's talk shows. The late-night programs have more important things on their mind, such as Madonna's underwear or the suicide of a troubled rock star. Yet some attention is paid to these issues in the more rarefied locales of the nation—the cozy diplomatic and foreign policy establishments, private and governmental, that generate the initiatives that eventually become the national foreign policy.

In the current era of eroding national authority, it is not too surprising that some policy thinkers and formulators have rediscovered the United Nations, which has existed for half a century. Its most powerful member has bypassed it for most of that time, but as a result of the changed international scene it has drifted back into at least a blurry focus for some national influence-wielders. Yet the UN, since its inception, has always presented a problem to U.S. diplomats. It is an *inclusive* body. Its membership includes the representatives of *all* but a few of the nations in the world. In these circumstances how can one, or a handful of still imperially minded societies, allow 185 national voices to participate in governing the world?

The original design of the UN tried to overcome this "obstacle" by locating major decision authority in the Security Council, which is dominated by a small club of the most powerful states. Still, this too proved an unacceptable limitation on United States' postwar aims, especially with the presence on the Council of a rival nonmarket society armed with atomic weapons.

In the early days of the United Nations, with a few exceptions, there was almost constant deadlock. The creation of NATO (the North Atlantic Treaty Organization) and other regional alliances, served by design, to take away from the one truly international organization, its global role and importance. The frequent blockage of U.S. goals that the presence of the former Soviet Union in the Security Council created, received heavy U.S. media attention, though not clarification about the source of the disagreement—generally, U.S. unwillingness to allow the loss of any part of the world market economy. Instead, the fraught messages and scary headlines served effectively to convince Americans of the unreasonableness of the Russians, and, consequently, the need for a gigantic arms program.

The UN was deemed an unworkable organization by U.S. leaders for other reasons as well. The most important objection, rarely made explicit, was the presence of a large bloc of nations, the former colonial territories. These states, at least in their early postindependence years, constituted a majority, as well as a vocal opposition, to U.S. and Western efforts to retain, or reimpose, economic and cultural arrangements that perpetuated these nations' dependency. The clash of interests between the few highly industrialized and powerful states, with the United States acting as militant whip, and the overwhelming majority of "have nots," was epitomized in the struggle, first, for a New International Economic Order (NIEO) and, soon thereafter, a New International Information Order (NIIO). The West and the U.S. refused to allow changes in the prevailing world economic and cultural patterns that favored and perpetuated the interests of the "have nots."

The lesson Washington took away from these engagements, in the 1960s and 1970s, was to regard and treat the United Nations as an oppositional force. The UN, as a body inimical to American life, was a recurrent theme in the American media. In relatively few years, polls—undertaken by surveymakers who were often in close association with those who had created the hostile political atmosphere to the United Nations—would demonstrate that the American public wanted nothing to do with the UN. This "public opinion" became the justification for Washington's further anti-UN behavior. It was also a good example, so dear to the hearts of TV executives, of "giving the people what they want," *after* they have been repeatedly "informed" by the information managers.

The collapse and disappearance of Soviet power have made changes inevitable in the long-cultivated anti-UN outlook. Today there is only one superpower left (though the Russians retain enough atomic weaponry still to be considered something more than a defeated rival). A United Nations, with a supplicant Russia, instead of a veto-exercising superpower, holds more attraction to Washington strategists. Yet the will to dominate, without an international mediating body, remains strong in some sections of the governing elite. And so, there has been in recent years an alternating set of views, one of which expresses the desire to utilize the United Nations as an instrument for advancing U.S. *national* interests; another, laying out an uncompromising unilateralist position. In both outlooks, there is the assumption that state power remains in place, and will continue to prevail in the time ahead. This creates something of an air of unreality to both approaches but it does little to discourage their assertiveness.

The first option was signaled by a high-powered report from top international financial circles. A couple of months before the 1992 elections, while George Bush was still President, the Ford Foundation organized and convened an international advisory group to consider how the UN might be more effectively financed. Described as an "independent" body, the roster of the group, with a few minor exceptions, was a Who's Who of international capital. It was co-chaired and led by Paul Volker, former chairman of the Board of Governors of the U.S. Federal Reserve Bank, and the most influential U.S. financial figure in the Reagan years. The group also included Shijuro Ogata, a former Deputy Governor of the Bank of Japan and co-chair; the Vice Chairman of the Saudi International Bank; the former Prime Minister of France, Raymond Barre, who also was the Minister of Economy and Finance; the former president of the German Federal Bank; a director of the Bank of England, and other illustrious representatives of high finance.

The group saw as its task the revitalization of the UN in the post–Cold War era: It began its report with this statement:

> The world the United Nations was created to serve is entering a period of uncertainty, but also of great opportunity—a moment that resembles in many respects the brief and fleeting interval of hope which followed the Second World War. The end of World War II allowed the United Nations experiment to begin. Today, almost fifty years later, the end of the Cold War has at last made it possible for the UN to begin to function as the guardian of international peace and security its founders intended it to be.[14]

The conclusion of the study, in short, was that a Soviet-free UN now opens the possibility of organizing the world, without opposition, along market lines.

The significance of the project derived entirely from the fact that a group of very important representatives of global finance still believed that states participating in the United Nations could provide a viable means of organizing and stabilizing the world.

Not all were as sanguine. Another group was established by President Bush and members of Congress, the Commission on Improving the Usefulness of the United Nations. It produced a divided report in September 1993. A majority of the commission believed that the end of the Cold War created "a unique chance for a *United States–led* United Nations to fashion common responses to mankind's common problems."

Though this finding can hardly be regarded as an endorsement of internationalist thinking, it was found unacceptable by a minority of the commission. These members argued that "the post–Cold War world is [not] ready for a revitalized United Nations." Indeed, they maintained that the UN remains "largely in the grip of a substantial majority of dictatorial, authoritarian and statist regimes," and that "only rarely can the United States and its democratic allies build a constructive coalition in the face of this entrenched opposition."[15] Though a minority position in this particular commission, this view retains strong support in Washington policy making quarters. There are many variants of this outlook but there is one unifying sentiment: state power remains decisive in international affairs and, this being the case, the United States cannot yield its unilateral control over international affairs.

However weak the governing assumption of this view has become, one Washington voice after another incants the same message. Thus, a former Assistant Secretary of State and Ambassador to West Germany calls for "More Power to the Powerful," and asserts that "7 [a group of rich West European states, Japan, and the U.S.] is better than the UN's 181."[16] A former Assistant Secretary of Defense demands that we "bend the UN to our Will."[17] A former foreign policy adviser to Clinton's presidential campaign asserts: "Like it or not, we must lead."[18]

Somewhat more nuanced, but essentially in agreement with these views, is the prescription of Harlan Cleveland, an eminent foreign affairs voice throughout the post–World War II years, a former Assistant Secretary of State in the Kennedy Administration, and the U.S. Ambassador to NATO in the Johnson presidency. He recommends a "coalition of the willing," to run the world, in which the U.S. will be the most willing:

> . . . whether some Americans like it or not, the United States is still the only available chair of the executive committee for a club of democracies that calls the shots for world order, prosperity and development . . . the United States must lead by imagination, consultation, and persuasion, not just imagination backed by the power of the purse, Marshall Plan style. . . Those who have written off the United States of America as a has-been may be surprised by the story of international governance as it now develops.[19]

The top command of the foreign policy establishment, the President and his Secretary of State, are no less affected by an attachment to the "leadership syndrome." From the beginning of his Administration, President Clinton has emphasized, "we are, after all, the world's only superpower. We do have to lead the world."[20] And Secretary of State Warren Christopher said, "I think our need to lead is not constrained by our resources . . . I think that where we need to lead . . . we will find the resources to accomplish that."[21]

One glaring weakness of the "leadership" syndrome is Christopher's confident assertion of the resource capability of the U.S. to "lead" the world. This claim is precisely what is called into question by a Rand Corporation think tank analyst. To be a successful hegemonic power, and thereby maintain stability in the world

> is a wasting proposition. A hegemonic power forced to place such importance on military security must divert capital and creativity from the civilian sector, even as other states, freed from onerous spending for security, add resources to economically productive investments. As America's relative economic strength erodes, so does the comparative advantage over other powers upon

which its hegemony is founded . . . It is difficult to see, therefore, how capitalism can survive the decline of the Pax Americana.[22]

As if this were not enough bad news for those who look forward to a long era of U.S. world "leadership," a still greater problem confronts this expectation. No less far reaching is the condition that defines this historical moment: the reduced capability of *all* political formations—state, local, regional—to manage, much less control, the vast private economic forces that are now embodied in the transnational corporate system. (We leave aside here the impact on national governance of the renewed strength and clamor of nationalistic and ethnic forces in many parts of the world. These feed on the economic chaos produced by the global market system.)

This is no newly discovered situation, though the full political implications are not always made explicit, or maybe fully understood. It is noteworthy that President Clinton, in one of the earliest public speeches of his Administration, outlined succinctly the features of the present world order and some of the dilemmas they produced:

> Capital clearly has become global. Some three trillion dollars race around the world every day. And when a firm wants to build a new factory, it can turn to financial markets now open twenty-four hours a day from New York to Singapore.
>
> Products have clearly become more global. Now, if you buy an American car, it may be an American car built with some parts from Taiwan, designed by Germans, sold with British-made advertisements—or a combination of others in a different mix. Services have become global. The accounting firm that keeps the books for a small business in Wichita may also be helping new entrepreneurs in Warsaw. And the same fast food restaurant that your family goes to—or at least I go to—also may be serving families from Manila to Moscow, and managing its business globally with information, technologies and satellites.[23]

The President's sketch of the present global financial and industrial scene cannot be faulted. Though detailed transnational operations and business' efforts to maximize profits are left mostly unexamined, and the basic motivations of the system are cosmeticized, the description is accurate as far as it goes. And at least a trace of the effects of the operations of this private system are noted. "Could it be," the President asks, "that the world's most powerful nation has also given up a significant measure of its sovereignty in the quest to lift the fortunes of people throughout the world?"[24]

To this question, the answer is unequivocally "yes," but not for the reason Clinton offers. "Lifting the fortunes" of people around the world is hardly the motivation of the global corporate system now in place and which is reducing the authority of governments everywhere. Still, from this at least partial understanding of the workings of the global economy, the Clinton White House has come to one other fundamental conclusion. It concerns the role and importance of information in the routines and practices of the economic order. Here, too, the President's grasp of the new reality commands attention:

> Most important of all, information has become global and has become king of the global economy. In earlier history, wealth was measured in land, in gold, in oil, in machines. Today, the principal measure of our wealth is information: its quality, its quantity, and the speed with which we acquire it and adapt to it . . .[25]

It is this assessment that explains the genesis of the Clinton Administration's preoccupation with, and support of, the new electronic information infrastructure. It is the vast information capabilities that the new infrastructure will provide that excites the Government and that prompts the Presidential assertion that mastery of this technology will enable the U.S. "to win in the twenty-first century."[26] And for the moment, U.S. mastery of high tech prevails. A *Wall Street Journal* front page article on September 9, 1994, read: "A New Dominance: High-Tech Edge Gives U.S. Firms Global Lead in Computer Networks."

The reasoning is straightforward. If, in fact, information has become the vital element in the world (and domestic) economy, the expansion of information capability must confer increased and uncontested authority on those who have it. This conclusion reinforces the unilateralist position. Why offer support to the United Nations, or any other international body, if the means of global authority—information control—is at hand? But is it as simple as this? Those who believe state power will be enhanced with the new information technologies and expanded information flows may be overlooking one critical point. The main, though not exclusive, beneficiaries of the new instrumentation and its product, already are the powerful global corporations. As they have done in the past, they will be the first to install and use these advanced techniques. In fact, they have been doing so for some time.

The strength, flexibility, and range of global business, already remarkable, will become more so. The capability of the state, including the still very powerful United States, to enforce its will on the economy, domestic or international, will be further diminished. This may be partly obscured for a time because the National Security State will have at its disposal an enhanced military and intelligence capability, derived from the new information technologies. For this reason, the American state will be the least vulnerable, *for a time*, to the forces undermining states everywhere.

Interest rates, capital investment, employment, business-cycle policy, local working conditions, education, and entertainment increasingly elude national jurisdiction—as President Clinton intimated in his speech at the American University in 1993. Creation of a far-flung electronic information highway will accelerate the process. This suggests that the Government's information policy is a recipe for further diminution of national power. It will also encourage a still greater concentration of private unaccountable economic influence in geographically dispersed locales. Some see this as a development to encourage. Historically, the abuse of state power is given as the justification of this view. The state as a coercive force in history is hardly an arguable question. The issue today, however, must be seen in the power relationships that currently prevail. The national state always remains a potentially repressive force but now, private unaccountable economic power constitutes a greater threat to individual and community well-being.

The contours of the world-in-the making, of progressively enfeebled governments are, at this time, shadowy at best. But some forms and shapes of the future are at least discernible.

One description, heavily influenced by the role of the new information technologies, is offered by Alvin Toffler. He is one of the early boosters of the information-using economy and, accordingly, a darling of the neopopulist community as well as the mentor to Newt Gingrich, and has long called the current historical epoch the "Third Wave."[27] This represents, in his typology, the shift from an agricultural to an industrial and finally, to a information-using society. In this new era, according to Toffler in a 1994 interview, global organization, production, distribution, work, living arrangements, and war itself are all profoundly affected and changed. More cognizant than most of emerging realities, Toffler foresees the development of global "niche economies." Though not defined as such, these can only be understood as enclaves of successful transnational corporate activity, located in many places around the world. Some of the sites Toffler mentions include regions in southern China, parts of the former Soviet Union, the Baltic states, and southern Brazil. Actually, Toffler is identifying a distinctive feature of today's world, the sharp division between well-off and disadvantaged regions. This division occurs *between* and *within* countries, as we have noted earlier in the examples of India, Colombia, Mexico, and the United States. Now it is ubiquitous.

Though inequality in the social order is certainly nothing new, a late twentieth-century phenomenon, the "development" process that characterizes modern corporate activity worldwide, accentuates and deepens this condition. The new information technologies extend it further by providing additional capabilities—mobility, flexibility, instantaneity—to the global corporation.

Another more serious and comprehensive review of these developments is advanced in Saskia Sassen's work, *The Global City*. Sassen views the rise of what she calls global cities—Tokyo, London, New York, and lesser centers as well—as the direct outcome of the operations of the transnational corporations. These giant firms require a wide range of what Sassen calls "producer services," which can be located and concentrated in a few metropolitan centers. These include advertising, design, accounting, financial, legal, management, security, and personnel. The political, economic, and cultural effects of these new centers offer a glimpse of what the future may be like.[28]

For Kenichi Ohmae, writing in the *Wall Street Journal,* the future is already here.

> No longer will managers organize international activities of their companies on the basis of national borders. Now the choice will be not whether to go into, say, China, but which region of China to enter . . . [and] The primary linkages of these natural economic zones are not to their 'host' countries but to the global economy.

Ohmae finds that the best example of what he is describing

> . . . is Dalian, a prosperous city of 5.2 million people in Liaoning Province in northern China, Dalian's prosperity has been driven not by clever management from Beijing but by an infusion of foreign capital and the presence of foreign corporations. Of the 3,500 corporations operating there, as many as 2,500 are affiliates of foreign companies from all over the world . . . . In Dalian you can virtually smell the global economy at work.[29]

Some "niche economy"!

Additionally, Toffler's "niche economies," whose development he attributes to the effects of the new information technologies, contribute to what he terms the "Revolt of the Rich." This is a phenomenon that reverses historical experience. Revolts in the past invariably have been by the poor. In this era, well-off groups and locales want to preserve and extend their advantages. They do their best to separate themselves from and to discard their lagging and disadvantaged countrymen, regions, and states.

It is not necessary to fully endorse Toffler's explanation for this spreading development, but it does describe rather well the direction that can be detected *inside* the United States today, to say nothing of other areas and regions of the world. The poor, a good part of the minority population, and the inadequately educated, increasingly are being cordoned off in urban centers, jails, hospitals, and relatively inaccessible pockets of isolation. Similarly, privileged countries try today to seal themselves off from masses of desperate people who hope to escape from destitute home areas: Western Europe tries to keep Africans and East Europeans out; Japan maintains a tight control over immigration; Washington is wary of the human tide from the southern hemisphere that presses against the continental borders.

Can the rich enclaves, favored groups and still relatively viable if not successful nation states, succeed in severing their ties with their poor neighbors, in and outside, their borders? Toffler doesn't directly address this central question but he does speak about "niche war," and the connection is unmistakeable. The Persian Gulf War in 1991 is regarded as an early model of what may be in store for those seeking to challenge the new world corporate order.

> . . . if we are now in the process of transforming the way we create wealth, from the industrial to the informational . . . there is a parallel change taking place with warfare, of which the Gulf War gives only the palest, palest little hint. The transition actually started back in the late 1970s, early 1980s, to a new form of warfare based on information superiority. It mirrors the way the economy has become information-dependent . . . In military terms there will be attempts to coordinate all the knowledge-intensive activities of the military from education and training to high-precision weaponry to espionage to everything that involves the mind—propaganda—into coherent strategies.[30]

With "niche war" strategy, utilizing high-tech information capability to overcome social eruptions, Toffler also endorses, and enthuses over, along with many others, the transmission of news and information to disaffected areas. CNN for example, is regarded favorably as a suitable channel in such endeavors, as are the BBC and Japan's NHK. All of these are seen, apparently, as unproblematic reliable vehicles dispensing "news" and information that will undermine the dissidents, whoever they may be.

Washington's plan for an information superhighway does not explicitly mention these applications, but the thinking underlying the project surely takes them into account. What else can it mean when the installation of the new information technologies are regarded as the vehicle to "win in the twenty-first century?" But can precision warfare, with a high information component and control of global news flows, keep the world orderly while privately initiated economic forces are contributing to wildly disproportionate income distribution and gravely distorted resource utilization, locally and globally?

The deepening crisis that is provoked by advanced technology, used mainly for corporate advantage and brought into operation according to the rules of the market, may summon forth even less promising "solutions." Direct military interventions in nations "where governments have crumbled and the most basic conditions for civilized life have disappeared . . . is a trend that should be encouraged." writes one historian whose views have had respectful attention in the mainstream media. The root cause of the problems in many Third World countries, according to Paul Johnson, "is obvious but is never publicly admitted: some states are not yet fit to govern themselves."[31] This condition he sees as most evident in Africa.

But it is not a matter of being fit to govern oneself—a patronizing, if not racist, charge when applied to a whole continent (Africa). In the last years of the twentieth century, satisfactory governance is in crisis almost *everywhere*, though more apparent in some locales than others. It derives from the weakening of state authority, which has been brought about by half a century of Cold War conflict, and its machinations, in tandem with the expansion of unaccountable private economic power. Information technologies at the disposal of this power further exacerbate conditions. The response to this global crisis demands a totally different economic, political, and cultural direction to what now prevails. In the words of Harvard Professor Michael J. Sandel:

> Those in America who worry about the loss of sovereignty to GATT, or those in England who worry about a loss of sovereignty to the European Union, may seem at times like the king who stood on the beach and tried to stop the tide . . . But [they] have a point. These global markets are not accountable to any citizens. They don't necessarily reflect decisions that we have made on the basis of our collective values. One of the biggest challenges for democracy in our time is to develop political institutions that will be powerful enough to deal with global markets, but accountable enough to enable citizens to feel they are still in control.[32]

After experiencing the impact of market forces on the Mexican economy in December 1994, President Ernesto Zedillo echoed this conclusion:

> It is obvious that the speed at which international financial markets have evolved over the last twenty-five years has been much faster than the capacity of governments and international organizations to cope . . . Mexico was the first to pay for this problem.[33]

What Zedillo calls "international financial markets" are the movements of transnational corporate capital. Their freedom, and more precisely, their unaccountability, has been the single-minded objective of U.S. policy since the end of the Second World War. Only now are the consequences of what has been a very successful policy beginning to become observable.

Notes

1. Remarks of Vice President Al Gore, delivered at the meeting of the International Telcommunications Union, Buenos Aires, March 21, 1994. See also Nathaniel C. Nash, "Gore Sees World Data Privatization," *New York Times*, March 22, 1994, sec. C, p. 2.
2. The National Information Infrastructure, Agenda For Action, Executive Summary, Washington, D.C., September 15, 1993.
3. Herbert I. Schiller, *Mass Communications and American Empire*, revised edition (Boulder, CO: Westview, 1992).
4. Ibid., especially chapters 3 and 4.
5. World Investment Report, Transnational Corporations and Integrated International Production, 1993, United Nations Conference on Trade and Development, Programme on Transnational Corporations, United Nations, New York, 1993, 22–23.
6. Richard Barnet and John Cavenaugh, *Global Dreams* New York: Simon & Schuster, 1994).
7. Business Week, April 18, 1994, p. 134.
8. Ken Auletta, "The Magic Box," *New Yorker*, April 11, 1994, 40–45.
9. Ibid.
10. "As Prosperity Rises, Past Shackles India," *New York Times*, February 18, 1994, p. l.
11. James Brooke, "Colombia Booms Despite Its Violence," *New York Times*, February 10, 1994, sec. C, p. 1.
12. Paul Lewis, "U.N. Lists 4 Lands at Risk Over Income Gaps," *New York Times*, June 2, 1994, sec. A, p. 7.
13. Louis Uchitelle, "Is Growth Moral?" *New York Times Book Review*, March 27, 1994, p. 23.
14. Financing an Effective United Nations, A Report of the Independent Advisory Group on U.N. Financing, A Project of the Ford Foundation, February 1993, p. 3.
15. Paul Lewis, "U.S. Panel Splits on Ways to Improve the U.N.," *New York Times*, September 13, 1993. Italics added.
16. Richard Burt, "More Power to the Powerful," *New York Times*, May 14, 1993, sec. A, p. 15.
17. Richard Armitage, "Bend the U.N. to Our Will," *New York Times*, February 24, 1994.
18. Michael Mandelbaum, "Like It Or Not, We Must Lead," *New York Times*, June 9, 1993, sec. A, p. 7.
19. Harlan Cleveland, *Birth of a New World Order: An Open Moment for International Leadership* (San Francisco: Jossey-Bass, 1993), p. 223.
20. President Clinton, News Conference, *New York Times*, April 24, 1993, p. 5.
21. Steven A. Holmes, "Christopher Reaffirms Leading U.S. Role in World," *New York Times*, May 28, 1993, sec. A, p. 6.
22. Benjamin C. Schwarts, "Is Capitalism Doomed?" *New York Times*, May 23, 1994, sec. A, p. 11.
23. President Clinton's speech at The American University, February 26, 1993, text in *New York Times*, February 27, 1993, p. 4.
24. Ibid.
25. Ibid.
26. Agenda For Action, op. cit.

27. Alvin Toffler, *The Third Wave* (New York: William Morrow & Co., Inc., 1980).

28. Saskia Sassen, *The Global City* (Princeton: Princeton University Press, 1991).

29. Kenichi Ohmae, "New World Order: The Rise of the Region-State," *Wall Street Journal*, August 16, 1994, sec. A, p. 12.

30. "Shock Wave (Anti) Warrior," A Conversation of Alvin Toffler with Peter Schwartz, *Wired*, November, 1993, p. 64.

31. Paul Johnson, "Colonialism's Back—and Not a Moment too Soon," *New York Times Sunday Magazine*, April 18, 1992, p. 22.

32. Michael J. Sandel, quoted in *New York Times*, July 24, 1994, p. 3.

33. Tim Golden, "Mexico's New Leader Finds Job Full of Painful Surprises," *New York Times*, March 14, 1995, p. 1.

7

AMERICAN POP CULTURE SWEEPS THE WORLD

American Pop Culture Sweeps the World

Governability and economic stability, for most states, are increasingly problematic. The far-ranging activities of essentially stateless businesses undercut local decision making everywhere, a phenomenon some like to call "globalization." The central player in this process, one writer notes, "is the transnational corporation. The primary driving force is the revolution in information and communication technologies."[1]

The new information and communication technologies are indeed at the center of the current changes, providing the technological means for world businesses to conduct their operations. Equally important, they supply the cultural industries with the instrumentation for reaching global markets with their media-cultural product. Dense worldwide communication networks are now available for corporate (and other) use. The proposed global information infrastructure (see chapter 6) intends to extend the capacity and accelerate the speed of these linkages.

In these onrushing developments, meaningful input from the public sector is being foreclosed by a rash of corporately organized initiatives that are creating a de facto commercial framework for global communication. In 1993 and 1994, for example, in the space of months, the three major United States long-distance telecommunications carriers signed agreements with powerful European partners to stake out shares of the world communications business.[2]

These arrangements do not in themselves constitute a completed global information infrastructure. They supplement networks already in place. Their significance is that they underline the prioritization of private interests in the unfolding global system. "Industry experts," writes one knowledgeable telecommunications reporter, "say that all long-distance carriers are chasing a market of only about 2,000 corporate customers, most of which are either based in the United States or have some operations there."[3] Whatever the number of companies in this market, they represent a minute, but spectacularly influential fraction, of the global community.

Which particular telecommunications consortia will command the future global communications system remains to be seen. What is not in doubt is that whichever specific groups come to dominate the field, the steady erosion of national power will continue. Contrary to the view that anticipates a global civil society emerging—featuring diversity, and roughly equalitarian roles for participants—the evidence overwhelmingly points to a world order organized by, and in the interests of, large-scale private economic enterprises.[4]

The electronic communication infrastructure now being created is intended to serve these interests in two important ways: the information flows that are, and will be, transported over the network serve to command and rationalize economic activity, and to extend the reach of corporate marketing to every corner of the earth. The second, equally vital function of the communication infrastructure, is to provide the circuitry for the already immense, and still increasing, flow of the product of the (mostly but not exclusively) U.S. cultural industries. This flow circles the world. Its impact, in ways to be described, further weakens the influence of local leaderships, and thereby creates additional national and global instability.

The Global Reach of the Cultural Industries

"A Star Rises in the East," announces the largest and most influential newspaper in California. What is this new point of light in the universe? Is it seen over the U.S. eastern seacoast? Hardly! It is Star Television, a satellite television broadcasting company, based in Hong Kong and recently acquired by Rupert Murdoch, the Australian-English-American media mogul.

Star Television is transmitting programs, mostly but not exclusively American-made, in English, to thirty-eight countries, including Kuwait, South Korea, Thailand, Indonesia, Pakistan, United Arab Republic, Philippines, Saudi Arabia, Hong Kong, Israel, Taiwan, India, and China. At least 360 advertisers, a Who's Who of the transnational corporate world, use Star Television to get their messages to the people of Asia and the Middle East. The voices included are those of Audi, Canon, Coca-Cola, Hennessy, Levi Straus, MasterCard, Mobil, Motorola, NEC, Nike, Panasonic, Pepsi-Cola, Reebok, Sony, Sharp, Shell, and Toshiba.[5]

Mr. Murdoch, owner of Star Television and numerous other media enterprises around the world, it is discreetly noted, "is the prime illustration of how much of the diversity appears to be coming under the control of a few international giants—nascent global networks of a sort. Power is concentrating in the hands of those with the money, the experience and the programming to establish the big regional systems of today."[6]

Mr. Murdoch is not alone, although there is not necessarily a big crowd of competitors. American media giants are in the global arena, too. "Viacom, Time Warner, Turner Broadcasting and Capital Cities/ABC (now merged with the Disney Company)," it is reported, "have already entered the race in Asia . . . [and] are altering the viewing and spending habits of a continent that is home to two-thirds of the world's population and some of its fastest growing economies."[7] In China, in 1993, there were an estimated 500,000 satellite dishes in the country and "fifteen million subscribers to multichannel systems that import English-language programs."[8] These proliferating communication networks, and the programming they carry, contribute to the worldwide unravelling of political and cultural sovereignty. "Not only are governments increasingly giving up their control of the airwaves by privatizing their broadcasters and allowing commercial television," one reporter writes, "but satellite technology has largely made national borders irrelevant."[9]

The Political Role of the Global Media Industries

The consequences of global information mastery were strikingly on display throughout the Persian Gulf War. During the actual hostilities, one account—that of the transnational, U.S.-based and owned Cable News Network (CNN)—dominated television screens around the world.[10] One definition and one account of this momentous geopolitical event was given to global audiences. For the national public, it served as a chilling signal of how orchestrated and concentrated the information supply had become. Though press interpretations of the war may have varied from country to country, the vivid broadcast images of high technology combat were identical worldwide.

This particular demonstration of information monopoly was remarkable but it barely suggests the full dimensions of the capability to define reality now at the disposal of the largely U.S.-owned cultural industries, and by the BBC's World Television Service and France's Euronews. International broadcasting, and CNN's output in particular, are but one kind of image, sound and symbol production. Such output also comes in the familiar forms of film, television programs, video games, video cassettes, newscasts, recordings, CD ROMs, books and magazines, multimedia offerings, and, not least, electronic on-line data and computer software itself.

The special significance of the transmission of this diverse and rapidly growing production is succinctly explained by Walter Wriston, former chief executive officer of Citicorp, one of the global banking giants:

> The single most powerful development in global communities has been the satellite, born a mere thirty-one years ago . . . Satellites now bind the world for better or worse, in an electronic infrastructure that carries news, money, and

data anywhere on the planet at the speed of light. Satellites have made borders utterly porous to information.[11]

Wriston properly makes no distinction between news, money, and data: "[H]undreds of millions of people around the world are plugged into what has become essentially a single network . . . of popular communication."[12]

Those global corporations and media-cultural conglomerates that have the capability to use the global satellite systems are indifferent to formal communication boundaries. Digitized electronic communication transforms all messages and images into a uniform information stream. This globalization of communication since the 1960s is represented in the phenomenal growth of transnational media-information corporations such as Time Warner, Disney, Reuters, SONY, Murdoch's News Corporation, and Bertelsman. They are based mostly in the developed economies but their activity is worldwide.

While state, non-governmental, and non-corporate organizations have made use of the new electronic networks, their utilization is dwarfed by that of the transnational companies. The capability of the private, resource-rich conglomerates to transmit or shift messages and images, capital, currency, production, and data—almost at will—constitutes the true levers of contemporary power. For example, a world-class cultural industry corporation such as Time Warner or Disney, or one of Murdoch's enterprises, can combine a rich mix of informational, pop-cultural activities, synergistically spinning one product off another, or promoting one item by incorporating it in another format. Novels, in some instances, become movies. Movies wind up as TV series. TV programs and movies are retailed as video cassettes and their sound tracks move out into their own orbits as records and tapes.

To top it off, sophisticated management of a conglomerate like Disney, engages as well in retail business, selling its various creations and promotions that originated as film or television, in shops owned or franchised. The release of Disney's animated film *The Lion King*, for example, in the summer of 1994 was a resounding hit and brought all of these corporate interconnections into play. There were tie-ins with Burger King, Toys Я Us and Kodak.

> The movie is the hub of a marketing program that connects its book, movie, recording, and theme park units . . . In addition, Disney has its own spinoff products from the movie. It has shipped more than a million books to retailers, and last week *The Lion King* soundtrack landed at the top of the Billboard charts when it sold 271,000 copies . . . Disney expects all of the cross-promotion to bring people to its 200 retail stores . . . and the company has created special promotions tied to the movie to keep the cars coming to Disneyland, which now has a *Lion King* parade.

The benefits of such corporate synergy are estimated at $1 billion in profits over two or three years.[13]

The net effect of such total cultural packages on the human senses is impossible to assess but it would be folly to ignore. For example, transnational polling companies, also mostly U.S.-owned, make surveys of audiences that have been exposed to transnational advertising and commercial programming. In one poll, data was assembled and tables constructed on "What People Think They Need." The North American Free Trade Agreement (NAFTA) received some of its support in Mexico, this survey indicated, from the people's "Hunger for U.S. Goods," seen "on imported television programs and in movies."[14]

The worldwide impact of the transnational cultural industries, it can be argued, may be as influential as other, more familiar, forms of (U.S.) power; industrial, military, scientific. In recent years it has actively abetted the transformation of broadcasting and telecommunications systems around the world. People everywhere are consumers of (mostly) American images, sounds, ideas, products and services.

Former Citicorp CEO Walter Wriston enthusiastically makes clear that national efforts to protect and insulate a community from these stimuli have been futile. Not unexpectedly, therefore, global notions of what constitutes freedom, individual choice, a good life, and a desirable future come largely from these sources. Institutional infrastructures in country after country have been recast to facilitate the transmission of the informational and cultural product that pour mainly from American cultural enterprises. Inexorably, from the initial conception and the first design, to the ultimate product, market criteria and imperatives prevail in the cultural factories and their outputs.

Media analyst Edward Herman describes the integration of broadcasting into a global market in recent decades, achieved largely through "cross border acquisition of interests in and control of program production and rights, cable and broadcasting facilities and the sale and rental of program stocks, technology, and equipment."[15] These are practices and activities that duplicate the expansion programs and financial legerdemain of other manufacturing or service enterprises in the global market place.

However, there is at least one critical difference in the media-informational sphere that distinguishes it from the rest of the for-profit industrial system. This is its direct, though immeasurable, impact on human consciousness. What is standard economic behavior for media-cultural companies, therefore, rarely fails to have considerable socio-cultural impact as well. For example, the international economic expansion in broadcasting that Herman writes about, "[has] tended to increase the strength of commercial broadcasting and reduce that of public systems."[16] Herman concludes that "The strength and momentum of the forces of the market in the last decade of the twentieth century are formidable. It therefore seems likely that the U.S. patterns of commercial hegemony over broadcasting will be gradually extended over the entire globe."[17] This is no minor change! Half a century's experience demonstrates that commercial broadcasting transmits images and messages vastly different from those produced by a public service broadcasting system.

Herman's predictions have been validated with astonishing rapidity and singular effect. While American cultural product—film, television, fashions, and tapes—still dominate screens, homes, and shops throughout the world, local and regional outputs also are increasing. Invariably, however, they are fashioned on the American model and serve the identical objectives of the original. They are commercial products designed as bait with which to snare the potential consumer. French TV dramas, for example, repeat worn U.S. formulae; British producers are no less compelled than their American counterparts, to concentrate on audience ratings; Brazil's powerful television production industry is at the beck and call of the same transnational advertisers who dominate North American television screens.[18]

The American pop cultural product has obviously attractive features that can be attributed to a century of marketing experience and the rapid utilization of state-of-the-art technologies to achieve compelling special effects. These developments, coming at the end of the twentieth century, should serve as an alarm signal. The globalization that many find such a promising prospect can be viewed more realistically as the phenomenally successful extension of marketing and consumerism to the world community. A world communication infrastructure, heavily dependent on the new information technologies—satellite, computer, fiberoptic cable—is being put in place. It serves largely the needs of global business, engaged in producing and marketing its outputs worldwide.

Other constituencies, to be sure, also use these new electronic networks. Non-governmental organizations, professionals, social groups, and individuals, each have some access to the instrumentation. Clearly, this global and local "civil society" has had its expression and activities enhanced and facilitated with such facilities as the Internet. Yet the balance of advantage in the utilization of these networks is hardly equal. The efforts of the noncorporate users remain puny and relatively marginal. The Internet itself is all too likely to be transformed into a commercial and pay-for-use system in the near future.

The Flattening of Public Debate

In one respect especially—access to the media—the disparity in influence is overwhelming. For many years this has been particularly observable in the United States. Now it has become characteristic of global affairs.

In the United States, despite a seemingly thick network of organizations and social groups that make up a rich civil society, the voice of the corporate speaker has succeeded in dominating the national discourse. Although the corporate perspective has for generations held a privileged place in American society, it was balanced in earlier times by the opposing voices of farmers' movements, organized labor, and civil rights organizations on the national stage. Since the end of World War II, powerful structural changes have transformed the American economy and weakened, if not eliminated, most of these dissenting voices. Additionally, the arrival of television in the same period, has also contributed to the near-disappearance from the American scene of a national and comprehensive adversarial view.[19]

Single-issue constituencies have emerged and their oppositional voices occasionally receive prominence, and from time to time some issues do generate a modicum of excitement. For the most part, however, consensuality prevails on the essential features of the social order. The main business of corporate America, money-making, proceeds uninterruptedly. So, too, fundamental institutions have been reshaped to accommodate the dominant presence of the corporation in American life, offering thereby, seeming confirmation of the claim that what exists must be the outcome of inescapable natural forces.

Corporations not only enjoy the protection of the law. For more than a century they have been regarded and treated as *individuals*.[20] In the post-World War II period, the corporation has had its status further up-graded. Now it is granted substantial First Amendment rights.[21] These judicial interpretations have legitimized the preeminent role of corporate expression in the contemporary cultural landscape. Given the near-total dependency of American radio and television on commercial advertising, the domestic informational system has become, in effect, a marketing and ideological apparatus of hard-to-exaggerate influence. Only the largest national companies can afford to pay for prime time commercial messages and the programming that accompanies them. Corporate expression has no competition—literally.

Public broadcasting, which was supposed to be a noncommercial alternative to advertiser-supported television has been co-opted by sponsorship. This development has progressed to the point where the editor of *Harper's Magazine*, unqualifiedly, has called for the plug to be pulled on public television.[22] Paradoxically, despite its present conservative character, congressional rightwingers are doing their utmost to do just that—eliminate the system entirely. Cable television, while still receiving most of its revenues from paid subscriptions, is steadily drawing more support from advertisers as well.

In this political economy of communication, where revenues come exclusively from advertising, the quality of television programming, with some notable exceptions, falls far short of its informational-cultural potential. The commercial broadcasters' seemingly unlimited greed, expressed in their efforts to capture as large as possible a share of an increasingly fractionated audience, is a guarantee of cultural default—all too frequently in evidence. The absence of programming that might shed some light on the country's deepening general social crisis does not seem to concern the industry's owners. Instead, the audience is regaled with endless hours of sports spectaculars, fortuitous human tragedies, and infomercials.

In sum, with numerous nondramatic institutional changes, the economy, and cultural expression itself, have become the private domain of a highly concentrated transnational corporate power. As might be expected from this state of affairs, the realm of permissible debate has narrowed appreciably in recent decades. In the medium that really matters, television, there has been a proliferation of talk shows, call-in shows, and personal witness programs.

Though there are more television channels than ever and a large number of computer bulletin boards have been created where views are easily expressed and exchanged, for all this, the *national* discourse, where it exists at all, is astonishingly bland, where it is not raucously conservative. Scrutiny and debate about the structural determinants of American existence are nowhere to be found, at least not in the national media.

It follows that the rich fabric of American history, from colonial days to Clinton's presidency, with its never ceasing struggles against plutocratic privilege, and its strivings for social dignity and equality for working people (including women and African- and Mexican- and Native-Americans), rarely if ever, is brought to the attention of the national audience. Generally, what little that does get noted is either decontextualized or fragmented.

Globalization of Commercial Messages and Images

This thin and largely expurgated presentation of the national experience is the underside of the daily retailing of corporate images and messages and endless affirmations of commercial culture. In recent years these highly selective accounts no longer are confined within national boundaries. With the phenomenal growth of the transnational business system, and its utilization of the computer and the communication satellite, what used to be national in form and content has become transnational or, as some prefer to describe it, global. Additionally, the collapse of the former Soviet Union and the Eastern European political systems and the market "reforms" in China have opened a vast new terrain to transnational marketing and the corporate voice. The media-cultural conquest of these areas, for the moment at least, appears to be unconditional.

As early as September 1991, it was reported that in Moscow, "most of the fare at the movie theaters is now American . . . more than twenty American films are now showing in the city . . . [and] the brooding statue of Pushkin is bathed in the neon glow of a Coca-Cola billboard and the lights from the world's largest McDonald's restaurant."[23] Since this was reported, the Moscovites have lost their ranking as the site of the largest McDonald's. This status now is held in Beijing. Where it will be located next depends on the rapidity and breadth of the transnational corporate global envelopment.

With no significant oppositional pole to the transnational system now in existence, the poorer and weaker countries are almost defenseless against the economic and cultural maneuvers of the world business system. In fact, many of these countries' leaders have jumped enthusiastically on board, expecting to extract some marginal benefits for a tiny stratum (including themselves, of course) of their societies.

Mexico serves as an exemplary, though not unique, case of a country whose material and nonmaterial substance are being appropriated. The plans of one of Mexico's current big investors are described:

> Call it Pepsi's Latin invasion. And it's not just tacos, and not just Mexico. Last month the company [Pepsico] announced a $750 million five-year assault in Mexico, including plans to buy interests in big bottlers, big distribution routes and advertise heavily. The company is opening Pizza Hut, Taco Bell and KFC (Kentucky Fried Chicken) franchises throughout Latin America, and selling Fritos, Ruggles, and Doritos as far south as Tierra del Fuego. And it will soon announce that later this year it will spend tens of millions of dollars to sponsor Michael Jackson on an eight-city tour of Latin America.[24]

What is not in doubt in this account is the powerful media-economic interlock that now characterizes the global corporate dynamic. Saturation advertising follows (sometimes precedes?) the corporate investment. What are the long-term effects of this particular case; unhealthful changes in the national diet; likelihood of a nonreversible shift away from a self-reliant agriculture; the bathing of the public's senses in commercial imagery receive scant concern and certainly are not subjects for debate on Mexican television, which is more commercially dominated, if imaginable, than the U.S. model.

Mexico's economic collapse in the winter of 1994–95 in no small way can be attributed to the (largely U.S.-produced) advertising that led to extravagant expenditures on, also largely American-made, consumer goods, financed by short-term foreign loans. Pepsico's strategies to penetrate the Mexican and Latin American markets are replicated by hundreds, if not thousands, of other companies, striving for their shares of the world market.

The efforts of these companies contribute to the current global environment of transnational corporate capitalism, which follows similar marketing formulas and voices a uniform rhetoric.[25] This includes the espousal and

protection of corporate speech. It justifies whatever programming is produced and transmitted as the proof of consumer choice and sovereignty. International efforts to combat or counter the now-pervasive condition of
corporate dominance have been defeated by the counterattack of the
transnational corporate order and its national surrogates.

The Decline, and Renewal, of International Opposition to U.S. Cultural Dominance

In the 1960s and 1970s, a group of postcolonial Third World states made
mostly rhetorical efforts to create a New World Information and Communication Order (NWICO) that challenged the Western—mostly American—
domination of world news, and information and cultural flows. In meetings,
resolutions and international forums, widespread opposition to prevailing
media-informational practices was expressed. These views were summed
up by Zimbabwean Prime Minister Robert Mugabe, a decade after the
NWICO movement. His statement retained relevance because the same
conditions prevailed.

> In the information and communication field, the Non-Aligned Nations and
> other developing countries are adversely affected by the monopoly which the
> developed nations hold over the world's communications systems . . . . The old
> order has ensured the continued dependence of our information and commu-
> nication infrastructures and systems on those of the developed nations. Such
> dependence constitutes a serious threat to the preservation of our respective
> cultures and indigenous life-styles.[26]

Third World efforts on behalf of the NWICO agenda crested in 1978; the
concept, however, was overwhelmingly rejected by the United States and its
few developed allies. Further, the unity of the dissenting majority was shat-
tered by a United States offer of limited assistance for a development program in communication technologies, calculated to win some Third World
support. This was an early instance of the argument that communication
technology, by itself, could transport a nation out of economic misery.

The carrot of technical assistance was complemented with a frontal assault
in the Western mass media on the United Nations Educational, Scientific and
Cultural Organization (UNESCO). UNESCO had been an important locus
for NWICO advocates.[27] The attack culminated in the United States with-
drawal from UNESCO in 1984.

This unilateral action was widely opposed by many professional organizations inside the U.S. but represented a major strategic goal of the Reagan
Administration—to browbeat the international community into accepting

U.S. global information policy in particular and U.S. foreign policy positions in general—and, for some years, this did result.

Yet in an ironic twist, many of the poor world's cultural concerns have reappeared in the 1990s, voiced often by industrially developed countries. They are especially observable, for example, in the French Government's and cultural community's resistance to the unrestricted flow of Hollywood product into that country. The inability of United States negotiators to prevail over French objections in the December 1993 GATT final treaty provisions marked one of the few setbacks, however temporary, in the U.S. cultural industries' global advance. The anxiety displayed in France, though perhaps stronger than elsewhere, is manifest in varying degree across Western Europe, Canada, and in the Middle East. It is especially evident in the efforts of the European Union to tighten restrictions on imported U.S. film and television programs.[28]

The Weakening of International Structures of Information Accountability

The pursuit of American global information dominance has resulted in additional initiatives that have crippled or eliminated several national and international agencies and structures that once served as partial shields against unlimited transnational corporate power. In Europe, for example, there has been unrelenting pressure to eliminate or marginalize the Post, Telephone, and Telecommunications entities (PTTs). These governmental bureaucracies, for all their faults and rigidities, at least represented in part, *national* public communication interests.

Stigmatized by their transnational corporate adversaries as coercive "monopolies," their authority has been steadily diminished by liberalization and privatization measures—advanced by the transnational corporate sector and its local allies. The PTT capability to monitor and prescribe the behavior of the communication companies operating in their national space has been largely lost and the survival itself of these public entities is threatened. The *Financial Times* describes the situation with manifest relish:

> The European Commission will soon decide whether to abolish the telephone monopolies which exist in most member states. Its decision will not only be a watershed for telecommunications but will also define its overall attitude to public monopolies [*sic*] . . . The Commission has already taken small steps down the path of liberalization . . . But Europe has already waited long enough and nothing less than full competition will do.[29]

"Full competition" in this context, signifies the relinquishment of national accountability to the play of market forces.

Another example of growing corporate authority over transnational information flows is the forced evolution of the International Telecommunications Union (ITU). Founded in 1865 as the International Telegraph Union, the ITU was renamed in 1932 and charged with regulating the international allocation of the radio spectrum. Recently, however, the ITU has been restructured in order both to diminish the possibility of its majority's influence, mostly poor countries, and to extend the voice of the private sector in its policy making.[30] In fact, the ITU's existence as a United Nations-specialized agency is being contested. A United Nations affiliation, no matter how tenuous, with its suggestion of accountability to an international public authority, is deemed threatening by the transnational corporate sector. One report, reflecting this corporate sentiment, wondered "what role the U.N. intergovernmental agency will play in an evermore commercial world."[31] Similarly, a spokesman for an international telephone company questioned "the role of an inter-governmental organization in a global business that is overwhelmingly a private sector business."[32] Still another voice in the same chorus admonished: "As more and more [of its] members become commercial, so must the ITU, all the way to the top."[33] The extent to which the transnational corporate sector has its way, works to strip erstwhile international bodies of their public character and function.

Further indicative of the onslaught against public scrutiny have been the corporate maneuvers in the sphere of international trade and commerce. A subject which is opaque in itself, has been made still more mysterious by constructing an almost impenetrable semantic category, "trade in services," in the General Agreement on Tariffs and Trade (GATT). GATT itself, has been reorganized and now exists as the World Trade Organization (WTO). New as it is, the WTO remains a Western-dominated body whose policies govern a large part of the world's trade. Approval in the United States for the new organization, the *New York Times* reported, was pressed by "the nation's biggest businesses and agricultural groups . . . Its defeat, [they warned] would jeopardize America's efforts to lead the world economically at a time when the nation's military power is diminishing in importance."[34]

The creation of the obscurantist trade-in-services category was intended to safeguard from general knowledgability, and possible criticism, the increasingly important sphere of electronic data flows, including intellectual property data. These have become the primary pillars of transnational corporate power.[35] Writing from a perspective of centuries of colonial oppression, Chakravarthi Raghavan explains this seemingly benign linguistic move and the locus of its implementation:

> . . . among all the fora for dealing with such issues, the Third World countries
> are the weakest inside GATT, in terms of collective organization and bargain-
> ing . . .unlike UNCTAD, UN or other parts of the UN system, inside GATT

there is only a tenuous informal group of less developed contracting parties [countries] that meets from time to time to exchange information . . .[36]

The extreme sensitivity of the corporate order to the global information climate was also demonstrated by the successful effort to expunge the subject of transborder data flows (TDF) from the language and the agendas of international economic meetings. For a brief period in the 1970s, TDF—the term for mostly electronic data crossing national frontiers—was a subject of great debate. Yet its implications for the examination, and possible oversight, of the data flows of the global companies came too close to the nerve centers of the transnational business system. Because of this the term itself was neatly shelved and literally disappeared from the vocabulary of the international community. In its place emerged the less threatening, apparently innocuous, trade-in-services term and category of the GATT.[37] Almost overnight, the focus on global data flows vanished.

Having neutralized or eliminated international and state institutions of oversight, the communication super companies can carry on their worldwide operations, almost completely relieved of scrutiny. Domestically, their overseas activities are mostly ignored. Rare is the politician who mentions transnational corporate matters. International organizations like the United Nations, the ITU, UNESCO and the former UN Center for Transnational Corporations have either been bypassed, restructured, weakened, or neutered. The fate of the former UN Center for Transnational Corporations is especially illuminating. Established largely as a result of Third World insistence, the Center devoted its energies to making studies and issuing reports on the activities of transnational corporations. Apparently even this mild informational responsibility was too disturbing to the transnational corporate sector. In 1992, in one of its last newsletters, the Center announced its new status:

The Center on Transnational Corporations and the United Nations Division of Development Administration will now work together as the Transnational Corporations and Management Division. One of eight units in the United Nations Department of Public Economic and Social Development, the new Division will build on existing complementarities to strengthen *the move to market forces*.[38]

No authority in the international arena now exists to question, much less check, the actions of the prevailing transnational corporate order. In individual nation-states, the information and communication terrain has been made fully accessible to corporate messages, images, and data. These are protected under the expanded definition of free speech.

How have these developments affected the private international media organizations that now produce and manage the worldwide message and

image flow? Are these powerful cultural-industrial conglomerates independent and free standing? Do they pursue their own agendas, exclusive of
other interests? How do these agendas relate to the interests of generalized
transnational corporate power?

The main transnational media-information players today are not a second
string team of corporate actors. Time Warner, Disney, Microsoft, Reuters,
SONY, Murdoch, Bertelsman, to name just a few, are multibillion-dollar
enterprises, whose activities and outputs span all spheres of communication
and popular culture. Though each transnational company has its own specific interests, requirements and history, which defy generalization, *there
are still fundamental commonalities* that sometimes unite them.

For example, the demand for a new international information order was
a prominent issue in the 1970s, the treatment of that issue in the United
States media, *without exception*, was uniformly hostile.[39] Again, when the
United States Government put half a million troops in the Persian Gulf region in 1991, the national informational system closed its ranks—there
were a few marginal dissenting voices—and unqualifiedly accepted and en-
dorsed that decision.[40]

The record suggests that issues of high systemic importance receive immediate attention and support from the media combines. No less well protected and defended are the media's own interests, as they interpret them,
i.e., to delegitimate the call for a new international (or national) information
order; to protest as denials of free speech and free flow of information, the
European Community's limited effort to reserve some screen time for the
region's own film and television production. Most events and policies, however, are not of high urgency, demanding systemic attention and priority.
Countless unremarkable developments transpire daily and fall within the
general routines and permissible boundaries of "independent" interpretation. Crisis periods excluded, the international flow of messages and images
therefore, is not a systematically coordinated stream that receives approval
from some transnational corporate oversight board. Actually, such detailed
supervision is hardly feasible or necessary.

The standard procedures for selecting and removing individuals who
make the daily (hourly) news and programming decisions are not foolproof
but they are reliable enough (see chapter 1). The education of journalists,
their on-the-job training, and the recruitment and apprenticeship of cultural
taste-makers are not random processes. Large-scale media-cultural organizations, like other big enterprises, do not hire and assign personnel willy
nilly. The main newspapers, for example, in the Cold War years, did not
send correspondents to Moscow without prior vetting. Similarly, high-level
political appointments are automatically preceded by an FBI check.

The machinery of information control may not perform perfectly, but it
works quite well. In the 1990s the production, processing, and dissemina-

tion of information have become remarkably concentrated operations, mostly privately administered.[41] The major producers and distributors are key players in the domestic and transnational corporate worlds. Major television anchors, highly visible national correspondents, and top editors and publishers of the "quality" press turn up regularly as guests at White House dinners and other social functions. They are well aware of their individual company interests and are no less alive to the general stakes in the global corporate game.

Media and cultural power, awesome already, is further enhanced by its capability to define and present its own role to the public. This self-constructed picture never fails to emphasize the objectivity, dedication to the public interest, and alleged vulnerability of the cultural industries' activities. It does not follow that the general public accepts these media self-portraits. Still, does it really make any difference in most people's lives that one national cultural-informational institution after another is privatized and commercialized and that transnational media take over individual, national, and regional space?

The first, and most direct cost may be to the cultural work force itself. Reducing, and sometimes eliminating, state support for film, broadcasting, telecommunications and the arts in general, means less work in some cultural fields and more carefully monitored work in others. The plight of drama in the United States is suggestive of what may be expected of privatized arts activity, left to the play of market forces. In 1988 and 1989, for example, only thirty-eight per cent of the members of Actors Equity, the actors' union, worked at all during the year. Actors worked an average of seventeen weeks. Average salaries for actors were at poverty levels. Taking these grim conditions into account, one drama critic advised: "If you want to act, learn to type."[42]

The employment situation is not very different in other creative fields. Driven by the market, commercially-supported arts, sports, and entertainment produce poverty levels of existence for a majority of the creative and performance work force, alongside super salaries for a relatively few "stars." Much more difficult to estimate are the social costs to the community that accompany sweeping commercialization of the arts and the unrestricted entry of transnational entertainment and media conglomerates to national space. Indigenous creative forces are swamped and inevitably crippled by the relatively cheap cultural products offered by the big producers. The production quality of the material is also difficult to match because the producers allocate huge resources to the packaging side of the product—the sound, color, music, special effects, photography, and so on. The substantive component, the content, can be almost negligible alongside such fancy wrapping.

The heaviest cost of transnational corporate-produced culture, however, is that it erodes the priceless idea of the public good, the vital principle of social accountability and the longtime dream of international community. Substituted for these elemental human aspirations is the promise of consumer choice—a choice that is not genuine—and a hopelessly narrow standard of production efficiency.

Can the well-being and the vitality of any community be left to the international business system, especially its powerful media/entertainment sector? Canada's experience is cautionary. The United States' northern neighbor, with whom it shares a 3,000-mile border, has felt the full impact of the U.S. cultural industries. One Canadian, in a position to know, sums it up:

> From my Canadian point of view, [the unrestricted operation of market forces] have delivered a whole nation into cultural bondage, to the point where Canadian voices have been drowned out of their own air.[43]

Canada, we may be reminded, is no less industrialized than most European states.

Publicly unaccountable media-cultural power today constitutes the ultimate Catch-22 situation. The public interest, locally and globally, demands honest messages and images. These, however, are dependent on private media providers, whose own interests are often incompatible with the public's.[44] Private information monopolies are contributing, by their fierce, and to date successful, opposition to social oversight, to the growing global and national crisis of governabiity. This is the challenge of the time ahead.

Notes

1. Sylvia Ostry, "The Domestic Domain: The New International Policy Area," *Transnational Corporations*, Vol. 1, No. 1 (February 1992), p. 7.
2. Edmund S. Andrews, "AT&T Finds 3 Partners in Europe," *New York Times*, June 24, 1994, sec. C, p. 1.
3. Ibid.
4. Mike Featherstone, ed., *Global Culture* (Newbury Park, CA: Sage, 1990).
5. Christine Coutney, "A Star Rises In The East," *Los Angeles Times*, May 11, 1993.
6. Richard M. Stevenson, "Mondo Murdoch," *New York Times*, May 29, 1994, sec. 4, p. 1.
7. Philip Shenon, "A Race to Satisfy TV Appetites in Asia," *New York Times*, May 23, 1993, sec. F, p. 12.
8. Patrick E. Tyler, "CNN and MTV Hanging by a 'Heavenly Thread'," *New York Times*, November 22, 1993, sec. A, p. 4.
9. "Mondo Murdoch," op. cit.
10. Hamid Mowlana, George Gerbner and Herbert I. Schiller, *Triumph of the Image: The Media's War in the Persian Gulf: A Global Perspective* (Boulder, CO: Westview Press, 1992).

11. Walter B. Wriston, *The Twilight of Sovereignty* (New York: Charles Scribner's Sons, 1992), p. 12.
12. Ibid., p. 130.
13. Sallie Hofmeister, "In the Realm of Marketing, the *Lion King* Rules," *New York Times*, July 12, 1994, sec. C, p. 1.
14. Anthony DePalma, "Mexico's Hunger for U.S. Goods is Helping to Sell the Trade Pact," *New York Times*, November 7, 1993, sec. 4, p. 1.
15. Edward S. Herman, "The Externalities Effects of Commercial and Public Broadcasting," in K. Nordenstreng and H. I. Schiller, eds., *Beyond National Sovereignty: International Communications in the 1990s* (Norwood, NJ: Ablex Publishing Corp., 1993), pp. 108–109.
16. Ibid., p. 108.
17. Ibid.
18. O. S. Oliveira, "Brazilian Soaps Outshine Hollywood: Is Cultural Imperialism Fading Out?" Paper presented at the meetings of the Deutsche Gesellschaft fur Semiotik (German Society for Semiotics), Internationaler Kongress, Universitat Passau, October 8–10, 1990.
19. Herbert I. Schiller, *Culture Inc., The Corporate Takeover of Public Expression* (New York: Oxford University Press, 1989).
20. *Santa Clara County v. Southern Pacific Railroad*, 118 U.S. 394 (1886).
21. *First National Bank of Boston et al. v. Bellotti, Attorney General of Massachusetts et al.*, 435 U.S. 765 (1978).
22. Lewis H. Lapham, "Adieu, Big Bird," *Harper's Magazine*, December, 1993, pp. 35–43.
23. William E. Schmidt, "The Neon Revolution Lights Up Pushkin's World," *New York Times*, September 21, 1991.
24. Nathaniel C. Nash, "A New Rush Into Latin America," *New York Times*, April 11, 1993, sec. 3, p. 1.
25. Leslie Sklair, *Sociology of the Global System* (Baltimore, MD: John Hopkins University Press, 1991).
26. Speech delivered at the official opening of the Second Conference of Ministers of Information of Non-Aligned Countries, Harare, Zimbabwe, June 10, 1987. A good summary of NWICO argumentation and positions can be found in "Many Voices, One World," International Commission for the Study of Communication Problems (New York: Unipub, 1980).
27. William Preston, Jr., Edward Herman and Herbert I. Schiller, *Hope and Folly: The United States and UNESCO, 1945–1985* (Minneapolis, MN: University of Minnesota Press, 1989).
28. Roger Cohen, "Aux Armes! France Rallies to Battle Sly and T. Rex," *New York Times*, January 2, 1994, sec. H, p. 1. Also, Tyler Marshall, "EU Film, TV Leaders Meet to Try to Save the Industry," *Los Angeles Times*, July 1, 1994, sec. D, p. 4, also, Alan Riding, "European Union Proposes New Rules to Tighten Quotas on Foreign TV Programs," the *New York Times*, March 23, 1995, sec. C, p. 7.
29. "Free Speech in Europe," *Financial Times*, February 4, 1993.
30. Eileen Mahoney, "The Utilization of International Communication Organizations, 1978–1992," in Nordenstreng and Schiller, pp. 314–34.

31. Malcolm Laws, "ITU to Reorganize," *Communications Week International*, January 18, 1993, reproduced in *Teleclippings*, International Telecommunications Union, no. 901 (February 1993), p.4.
32. Ibid.
33. Ibid.
34. David E. Sanger, "Senate Approves Pact to Ease Trade Curbs; A Victory for Clinton," *New York Times*, December 2, 1994, p. 1.
35. Chakravarthi Raghavan, *Recolonization: GATT, the Uruguay Round and the Third World* (London: Zed Books, 1990).
36. Ibid., pp. 60–1.
37. William Drake, "Territoriality and Intangibility: Transborder Data Flow and National Sovereignty" in Nordenstreng and Schiller, pp. 259–313.
38. *Transnationals*, quarterly newsletter of the Center on Transnational Corporations, March 1992, p. 1, italics added, quoted in Colleen Roach, "Trends in Global Communications," Paper presented to the annual meeting of the International Association for Mass Communications Research (IAMCR), Guaruja, Brazil, August 20, 1992.
39. Preston, Herman and Schiller, op. cit.
40. Mowlana, Gerbner and Schiller, op. cit.
41. Ben Bagdikian, *The Media Monopoly*, 4th ed. (Boston: Beacon Press, 1992).
42. Dan Sullivan, "Unemployment . . . ," *Los Angeles Times*, December 23, 1989.
43. Bernard Ostry, "The Risk of Going Global," *New York Times*, December 31, 1989.
44. C. Edwin Baker, "Advertising and a Democratic Press," *University of Pennsylvania Law Review* 140, no. 6 (June 1992), pp. 2097–243.

8

THE "FAILURE" OF SOCIALISM AND THE NEXT RADICAL MOMENT

The "Failure" of Socialism and the Next Radical Moment

Today from West to East the end of Communism is hailed. If unrestrained triumphalism is absent in the West—e.g., "We Won" signs on national highways—there is an unmistakeable sentiment in opinion-shaping circles that no serious alternative now exists, *or can be contemplated*, to prevailing Western institutions.

The creation of an ideology of "no alternatives" is already well advanced in the Western world, and in the United States in particular. Its formulation can be said to have begun in 1990 with the widely heralded thesis—given enormous publicity in the U.S. media—about the "end of history." Francis Fukuyama, a former State Department official, concluded, actually somewhat wistfully, that the class struggle no longer mattered, and that all that was left for the present and future generations was a boring, liberal incrementalism.[1] Today, for the first time since the publication of the *Communist Manifesto* nearly a hundred and fifty years ago, the "specter haunting" Western capitalism seems to have been exorcised.

For the moment at least, the ideology of private ownership and individual acquisitiveness as the necessary and desirable motors of human development has prevailed. Actually, they have been reinforced. In erstwhile noncapitalist societies, as well as elsewhere, "market democracies" now exist or are well on the way to formation.[2] These, our foreign correspondents are fond of reporting, have stores and shop windows full of goods. This is the bright side of consumer choice. The side in the shadows is that a good part of the population in the new market democracies can only look at, not buy, the wares on display. In the construction of this post–Cold War consciousness, there are two interconnected themes: one is that socialism has failed. The other is that there are no alternatives to existing capitalism, so-called "market democracy." Let us examine these assertions in turn.

Has Socialism Failed?

Has socialism actually failed? Did the economies of Eastern Europe and the former Soviet Union, the African nonmarket societies, (Angola, Mozambique, Guineau Bissau, and South Yemen) the Latin American states (Chile, Nicaragua, and Cuba), the Asian anticapitalist states (China and Vietnam) collapse, or change direction, because of *inherent* weaknesses? Is central planning, to take one nonmarket organizing principle, incompatible with socially desirable productive growth?

Let us first set aside the hardly irrelevant question of how far did each of these societies stray from socialist principles. This must be taken into account at some point but it is not necessary now. It is sufficient for this analysis to insist that however removed some of the practices in these states may have been from a socialist ideal, they did attempt to organize their economies and their societies, on some nonmarket principles, varying from locale to locale. It is also incontestable that because of these efforts they incurred implacable hostility from the world capitalist system, and its most powerful members in particular. And among these, none was more antagonistic than the United States, the global guardian of the world order from World War II on.

It will take time to sort out and seriously examine all the elements that have contributed to the current global ascendancy of market doctrine—not, one hastens to add, with explanations from conventional Western social science. Here, the most we can do is to start with a question fiercely debated early in the century. It was, and remains: can one country, starting from a relatively low level of industry, develop a social order fundamentally different from what exists in the dominant and prevailing world system? And, if the future of the nation state itself, today, is regarded as problematic, can local efforts to escape the strictures of global corporate capitalism be any more successful?

Seven decades of experience strongly suggest that such individual efforts national, or local, are incapable of resisting global systemic power. It is not so much that alternative routes and, more important, different destinations cannot be imagined. It is that they cannot be pursued successfully, at least not for any significant length of time. The dominant world order and its most powerful national components deny to any even mildly revolutionary society—be it in Europe, Asia, Africa, or Latin America—the autonomy and the economic breathing space to move out onto a truly different path. The sanctions imposed on those who try are material and ideological, and applied with deadly effect.

Materially, pressure is exerted in at least two ways. One, direct and brutal, withholds financial assistance desperately needed by an invariably on-the-edge community, attempting to radically change its social system. There is an overwhelming need for economic assistance in the period of transition from one form of economy to another. Unavailability, or denial, of aid or credit, at this point, leads inevitably and rapidly to fatal distortions in the new society. These are expressed in the political and cultural as well as the economic life of the country. The harshness of the austerity, necessarily imposed when outside help is unavailable, soon erodes the popular base of the society's leadership.

In Chile in 1971, for example, in the early and pitifully brief days of the democratically elected Socialist government of Salvadore Allende, his essentially reformist Administration was pleading for a small loan from one of the international financial organizations, which was controlled by its major contributors the United States and a couple of West European states. The purpose of the loan was to tide the country over during a period of major economic changes, one being the nationalization of the copper industry, formerly owned by a couple of U.S. companies. The sum requested, even by the standards of that time, was minuscule, in the range of $30 million. By American fiat the loan was refused. At the same time, the U.S. placed an embargo on the country's copper exports. Life for most Chileans became immeasurably more difficult. The "revolt" of the Santiago middle-class housewives against the regime in 1973, gleefully reported in the U.S. media as evidence of the "failure" of socialism, was the intended outcome of U.S. initiated financial sabotage abetted by extensive CIA machinations.

There are dozens of similar examples of funds withheld from weak societies seeking to change their economic dependency in the post–World War II. Contrast this harsh and punitive policy with the current, relatively lavish, provisioning of financial and material aid to those countries in Eastern Europe *moving away* from social planning and returning to the rules of capital, the market, in the organization of their economies. It was reported, for example, that in less than a year, "the total assistance pledged (by leading Western industrial countries) to Poland and Hungary now amounts to roughly $14 billion in direct aid, loans, credit, forgiven debts, and technical assistance programs, with the United States contributing $939 million."[3] Ironically, these recipients complain about the meagerness of the largesse. Moreover, they are relieved, from time to time, of their debt burdens.[4]

Withholding of international loans and credits to states that have been disrespectful to capital has been the "gentle" option. Complementing the "let 'em starve" policy has been physical coercion—armed intervention, in its many guises. The Sandinistas in Nicaragua were compelled to spend their tiny resources combatting the "Contras," a U.S.-organized and financed insurgency. The Cubans, in addition to a thirty-year-old embargo, fought off a CIA-organized invasion at the Bay of Pigs and have been compelled to militarize their society to protect themselves against the fear of direct U.S. invasion. A part of their country continues to be occupied by a U.S. military base, Guantanamo, installed nearly a hundred years ago. Grenada, a tiny island state, also suffered a U.S. military intervention.

The former Soviet Union, from the time of its 1917 revolution, was a state under Western siege. German fascism was nourished by the West and directed against the East, with an estimated cost of twenty-five million lives to the former Soviet Union, along with a devastated land. The fighting had hardly subsided when the Cold War began. The arms race, ratcheted up by American initiatives and escalated to wild heights in the Reagan years, utterly drained the former Soviet society.

Still more destructive, if that is possible, has been the havoc wreaked on Vietnam by U.S. military and economic force. Leaving the country a shambles, maintaining a blockade until only recently (1994), the American media, all the same, shamelessly, have attributed Vietnam's impoverishment to the effects of socialism. Now that the country's leadership, essentially under duress, has indicated its willingness to reintroduce market arrangements—especially foreign private investment—news about that tortured land, in the American media, has been more frequent and more sympathetic. But not to the extent of informing Americans about the full dimensions of the catastrophe imposed on that society.

In Africa's few, initially socialistically inclined regimes, especially Angola and Mozambique, United States– or South African–sponsored and financed guerrilla movements (Unita and Renamo), have reduced these societies to starvation levels. When Zaire, one of the richest states in Africa, drained for decades by Belgian colonial interests, sought both independence and some approximate form of equalitarian society in the early 1960s, a combination of U.S. and West European interests, utilizing the machinery of the UN, killed Patrice Lumumba and installed their agent, Mobutu. Today, Zaire is a looted and despairing land. Western media reports *now*, after the fact, reveal the dictator's corruption and depredations.

The Western onslaught against material life in those countries trying to adopt nonmarket institutional arrangements has been fierce, unrelenting, and successful. Still, it does not fully explain why societies with revolutionary impulses have been so completely derailed from their newly chosen course. In at least some cases, an additional ingredient to physical deprivation and bodily harm contributed to breakdown. Here we encounter a second essential element, the consciousness factor, in explaining the "failure" of socialism.

The Formation of Consciousness

Were the initially radical societies, or at least their leaderships, capable of constructing a different consciousness in their people, one that could resist the blandishments of the products, *and the ideas,* of the most advanced capitalist economies? This would have required a totally different perspective about how people view the world and their place in it; the goals of personal life; what a society aspires to; and the ways that people relate to each other in work, play, and daily living.

Could, for example, a people be immunized against, or at least alerted to, the powerful messages and meanings carried in the West's seemingly innocuous consumer and entertainment products and technologies? How could the goals of a society be redirected from demanding personal gratification to the exclusion of community satisfaction? Is such a prospect attainable if the people are barraged with the products and images that define human freedom and welfare in units of material possessions and display behavior that disregards, and sometimes disdains, social responsibility?

Clearly, changing the constituents of consciousness is a daunting assignment. It involves far more than the intangible net of meanings that covers the realm of commodity culture. There are also the material elements that underpin and powerfully affect daily experience. These include the arrangements that structure work processes, i.e., who works, with what skills, under what conditions and for how much pay. How are these everyday circumstances affected by, or affect, gender, ethnicity, race? These are all crucial ingredients in the formation of individual consciousness.

How well did the late, nonmarket societies negotiate these vital social relationships? Not very satisfactorily, though not entirely deficiently. In this sphere too, however, the external dominating system imposed a fearsome set of limits on the entire nonmarket world sector. Shortages and unavailability of goods and services were common experiences, varying from country to country in the so-called "socialist bloc." These long-lasting austerity conditions in the nonmarket world contrasted dramatically with the decades-long boom in the United States and most of Western Europe after World War II. Affluent economies that excluded significant parts of their own population from the benefits provided a constant reminder of the deprivation existing in the nonmarket regions. Travelers' reports and television and film images of consumer well-being that filtered into these areas where shortages and scarcity were endemic could not fail to be compelling and unfavorable to the local scene.

There was a special irony to this. Many of these societies offered low-cost housing, free health services, cheap mass transportation, child care centers, abortion clinics, and price-controlled essential goods. These may

not have been of the highest quality but they were serviceable. The offerings, for the most part were *community* goods. Western reports either ignored or deprecated them. Most of those who received these services soon
came to take them for granted and resented bitterly the general inaccessi-
bility of individual consumer goods.

Especially susceptible to the lure of the living standards observable in the
West were the newly educated professional and administrative strata in the
former Soviet Union, China, and other state-managed economies. These
groups increasingly coveted Western styles and practices and consumption.
Though their privileges, relative to the rest of their societies, were substantial, they still felt denied. The externally imposed burdens—the armaments
race, trade, and financial embargoes—deepened the shortages in their
countries. In these same leading echelons, widespread acceptance of Western notions of individualism surfaced well before the later, large-scale, political upheavals. Instead of confronting these ideas and allowing a full
discussion of them—a national dialogue could only have had a salubrious
effect—there was suppression.

Individualism is one of the most powerful constructs of capitalism, its
theory elaborated by English writers centuries ago. It should not have
proved too difficult for the exponents of socialism to examine individualism, explain its origins, and offer historical evidence of its impact. Unin-
hibited individualism is hardly compatible with serious efforts to create
cooperative living patterns. The inability or unwillingness to consider, debate, and ventilate the issue indicated great weakness in the nonmarket
sphere's intellectual and political leadership. This weakness in the vital terrain of consciousness was fully exploited by the dominant world system and
turned against the nonmarket regimes with deadly effect.

Actually, the failure of the nonmarket societies to meet the ideological
challenge represented much more than intellectual weakness. It indicated
that the roots of capitalism, far from being extracted, were still intact and
the emergence of privileged classes well underway. This, and other factors
too numerous to detail here, added up to the collapse of whatever efforts—
and there were several—had been made to establish an alternative vision
and practice.

Lessons

What can be learned from these experiences and developments? One inescapable conclusion, already noted, is the heavy odds against a country
that is poor and peripheral, achieving a successful and long-lasting, class-
overturning revolution, one that creates sharply different socioeconomic
goals to those in the surrounding global system. The capability of that sys-

tem to enforce economic strangulation, to launch military interventions, to impose staggering arms burdens, and to wage an unending and extensive ideological war, seems to be a winning counterrevolutionary combination. Its success is evident in the defeat and collapse of the former Soviet Union, the reversion to capitalism in Eastern Europe, the continuing privatizing policy of the Chinese leadership, and, after decades of imposed harsh austerity, the increasing adoption of market behavior in Vietnam and Cuba.

It is equally apparent that the capability to adopt genuinely different social policies in countries subject to these pressures cannot be sustained—if initiated to begin with. An ecological approach to production, for example, as well as the pursuit of a standard of living that emphasizes basic needs, cannot be expected from weak, poor, and relatively unindustrialized societies. When such states are confronted by a powerful oppositional system of global dimension that uses every imaginable stratagem and practice to undermine the fragile alternative structures laboriously established, the outcome is inevitable. But it is not only nonmarket societies that have tried to escape the dominant world system only to face assault. Attacks have been mounted on such nations as Brazil, India, France, and Iran for attempting to secure limited sovereign jurisdiction over key industries—computers, film and television, oil. With rare exceptions, these countries have been forced to abandon their policies.

These realities, and other recent transnational corporate successes, seemingly herald the beginning of a long-lasting and unchallenged, era for a re-energized global capitalism. One after another, once powerful sovereign states have found their communication infrastructures divorced from national control. Transnational corporate decision making has replaced national sovereignty in a good part of the world. The North American Free Trade Agreement (NAFTA) and the European Union, foretell the advance of what some call globalization. More accurately, it can be viewed as the spread of unchecked transnational corporate activity and the retreat of national accountability.

Given these undeniable developments, the 1990s and beyond could be regarded as a looming golden age of corporate capitalism in which global resources are there for the taking by an unaccountable system of appropriation. But this would be seeing only one side of the current reality. Francis Fukuyama's *End of History* thesis notwithstanding, social conflict and upheaval are hardly diminishing. It is a daunting task to locate a single spot of stability across the globe, though admittedly some locales are less fragile than others. In the search for stability the American economy, the world's most powerful, is a good starting point because the United States exhibits the most mature characteristics of late twentieth-century capitalism. Additionally, and of the highest relevance to our general concern with information, the United States continues to be the world's foremost site of cultural production. Made-in-America messages circulate globally, capture the attention of world audiences, and far surpass any other country's output. American media are not bashful about this. The *New York Times*, for example in early 1994, carried this modest headline: "The New Colossus: American Culture as Power Export," and noted in passing that "of the world's 100 most attended films last year [1993], eighty-eight were American."[5]

The current global power position of American capitalism, and its media-cultural sector in particular, are easily demonstrable. All the same, can the United States be regarded as a stable society? The investing class, nationally and internationally, certainly has its doubts. How else to explain the massive capital flows churning the international financial system? And for good cause! U.S. annual trade and budget deficits amount to hundreds of billions of dollars. More telling still, the *internal imbalances* defy simple description, and deepen from year to year. The clash of economic interests, those with and those without resources, becomes increasingly strident but still veiled by political, electoral, and media mechanics.

Explosive as these economic disparities are becoming, they are over-shadowed by one cosmic peril that barely makes it into the media—or if it does, only in the most attenuated presentation. This is the environmental situation, seen in its broadest dimensions. How does the country's national leadership view America's connection to the planetary condition?

When George Bush was still in the White House, his chief of staff was John H. Sununu. Responding to a West European invitation, in the summer of 1990, to agree to common measures to combat global warming, Sununu asserted that "the issue is being addressed with a level of haste." According to a *New York Times* report, Sununu "opposed new emission limits contending that they would require major changes in the American way of life and the nation's industrial structure."[6] President Bush vigorously defended his deputy against those who criticized his environmental views: "These people are extremists. They just don't want us to grow."[7]

Sununu and Bush, in their way of seeing things, were right, as are their successors in the 104th Congress. Their reactions illuminate the market economy's unwillingness, even inability, to constructively address a life and death problem. Avoidance of planetary destruction *does require* measures that will interfere greatly with prevailing U.S. industrial and organizational processes *and with personal life styles as well*. And this imperative is not limited exclusively to the brazenly unaccountable American market system. Its applicability is worldwide.

Is it imaginable, for example, now in the mid-1990s, that the power holders in the United States, or Japan, or Germany, or even The "People's Republic" of China, would favor buses or, more shocking still, bicycles over automobiles? What would happen to General Motors, Toyota, and Daimler Benz? What would happen to the advertising industry that promotes these goods, and the banking system that finances their purchase? What would happen to the work force that produces the cars? Indeed, the summary dismissal of a good part of the work force that produced the ordinance for the Cold War—without any measures of assistance or new job prospects—provides the answer as to how a market economy treats working people. Profit-turning economic "growth," however damaging and exploitative of the planetary resource base, is the indispensable engine of all market economies, especially the most industrialized ones. (It also characterized those "socialist" economies that emulated Western methods.)

Predictably, the environmental sentiments of Bush and Sununu have not disappeared with the arrival of a new Administration in Washington. The Clinton-Gore White House is very emphatic about its dedication to "growth." In the Government's National Information Infrastructure program, the objective is put forth boldly: "The benefits of the NII for the nation are immense. An advanced information infrastructure will enable U.S. firms to compete and win in the global economy, generating good jobs for the American people and economic growth for the nation."[8] Less blatant perhaps than its predecessor, the Clinton-Gore Administration is no less committed to encouraging economic undertakings that will "win in the global economy" and thereby yield profits to investors, jobs to workers, and the primacy of American capitalism worldwide. Economic activity that takes into account the longterm well-being of the earth, and therefore, of everyone, everywhere, doesn't come into it.

Yet it is precisely this potentially fateful connection between systemically-driven, any stimulus-will-do growth—armaments, inane consumer products, high-tech glitz—and the health of nature, and consequently human health as well, that may be the ultimate barrier to the transnational corporate world-in-the-making. The grave economic and social problems that attend this thoughtless enterprise can only intensify and deepen an already pervasive crisis condition. This, then, is the context that suggests that it may be time to take a fresh look at an old proposition. A century or more ago it was theorized that capitalism would meet its end first in the country(ies) where the system was most highly developed. At that time these were England, Germany, and rapidly industrializing America. The experiences of the last seventy years give this hypothesis renewed credibility.

Today, the hope for a different social vision seems outlandish. A far-reaching ideological enterprise has worked effectively to spread acceptance of what is best. At the same time prevailing doctrine cultivates feelings of futility about serious change. Cultural and intellectual life is saturated with theories, messages, and images that deny or invert the historical dreams and aspirations of generations. In the current atmosphere, a social order in which personal goals could be accommodated to ecological realities, where individual gratifications could be tempered by community and social needs, where commodity production, instead of being expanded into all spheres of existence, would yield its place to an enlarged sector of activity governed by human connectedness, seems distant, if not chimerical, indeed.

But could it have been otherwise? And having failed up to this point in the last years of the twentieth century, are not such social visions likely to continue to elude poor and weaker societies in the immediate years ahead? Targeted for decades with the glitzy images of Western "development" that have carefully screened out its unattractive accompaniments, most people in most nations are intent on reaching similar levels of existence—with all the waste this promises and however unrealistic these goals may be. They are propelled along this course by their newly privatized economies and their absorption into the world marketing and advertising system.

In fact, these strivings are most strongly expressed in those countries that formerly practiced state ownership. A story from Russia in 1994 reports the ongoing disappearance of classical music radio stations in Moscow, "driven by advertising and money, radio here is beginning to bear a resemblance to stations in New York and Los Angeles, where classical broadcasts are under siege."[9] From China comes the news that its "airwaves are up for sale [and that] television and radio with their vast audiences are seen as a commercial gold mine . . ."[10] In these lands it is unrealistic to expect the immediate emergence of community-grounded, ecologically oriented production systems. The mood and politics of most of the leaders, not necessarily the people, in the former state-managed economies are reverential of the market—the very mechanism that intensifies the stresses on nature and has led to the present global environmental crisis. In other former colonial countries, the forces of privatization and the market are no less dominant

All this is not to suggest that social struggles in the world at large are on the wane. On the contrary! Sooner or later, probably sooner, all the continents will be swept by intense conflict, taking diverse forms. People everywhere will rebel at conditions that violate human respect and dignity. As the gaps widen between the privileged and the dispossessed in one country after another, and between countries as well, bitter and prolonged struggles may be anticipated, the inevitable outcome of market-led development. The rebellion in the poverty-stricken Indian state of Chiappas, Mexico, at the beginning of 1994 is a harbinger. Efforts of coalitions of the privileged to suppress these protests by what is now termed low-intensity warfare, as well as other means, may produce short term results. Yet the sources of the discontent will remain, to flare up again on other occasions.

Still, while the power of the dominant world system remains intact, it is unrealistic to soon expect *successful radical* outcomes in the poor parts of the world. Localized limited victories are imaginable. Far-reaching changes that overturn the social as well as the economic pillars of the established dominant order are most unlikely. The emergence of what could be called an ecological and transformational socialism, incorporating the long-ignored needs of gender, sex, and race, along with class, can not be expected, *at this time*, from the poorer parts of the world. This is true despite the widespread conditions of impoverishment and inequality found there.

It is revealing, for example, that among the many demands of the Chiappas guerillas was to acquire television receivers for the rural households in the Indian highlands.[11] While understandable, the request is tantamount to offering their adversaries, the Mexican transnational elite, access to the people's living space. The Indian leadership may believe that it can produce indigenous programming. The global experience demonstrates the difficulty of warding off the transnational cultural flow.

Where then might a successful transformational movement occur? Though some might regard it as another egregious example of Euro– or North American–centrism, the candidate put forward here is the United States. The U.S. has been the global *enforcer—referee* is an unacceptable description—of the world market system for fifty years. Today, the enforcer's role—financial leverage, military force, ideological mastery—must be shared, at least partially, with others; Japan, Germany, and whoever else gains commanding power, wield global authority.

Still, in the mid-1990s, it is the United States where decisive world power remains vested, but also where broad popular experience with the full-blown consumer society of spectacular waste, and the pervasive use of commercial imagery to extol it, are most widespread. It is in the U.S., too, that the word *stress* has general currency, and anxiety-reducing drugs (e.g., prozac) have millions of consumers, while an average family needs two wage-earners to cling precariously to the increasingly elusive American standard of living.

It is also in the United States where the public school system, at least for the children in the urban centers, and some others as well, is literally a holding operation. At the same time, the country's main and successful, though unacknowledged, educator is commercial television. Advertisements, mayhem, and sports engulf the audience, young and old alike. (Not content with an iron-clad commercial grasp on youngsters' minds, the latest "innovations" introduce TV commercials to public classrooms.)

It is in the United States, too, that the financial capability of billion-dollar corporations to buy broadcast time and newspaper pages to transmit images of their products and their self-promoting views, is justified, by them, as a constitutional right. Freedom of speech in America increasingly has come to mean the de facto dominance of corporate speech and corporate perspectives. It is also in the United States where smog hangs over many of the largest cities, and automobile traffic, featuring one-passenger travel in grotesquely high-powered vehicles, frequently backs up for miles on major highways, spewing deadly fumes into the already contaminated air. And it is in the United States alone, among advanced industrialized countries, where tens of millions are without health insurance.

None of these conditions of physical and social decay are exclusive to America, though they exist in the most intense and exacerbated form. In Europe and Japan, similar nightmarish developments are already observable. At the same time, and following the U.S. example, the European social services net is being cut away. The French monthly paper, *Le Monde Diplomatique*, for example, recently described the unravelling of *l'etat provenance*, the Welfare State in France.[12]

How can the foregoing litany of social breakdown in America at the end of the twentieth century be a source of hope for a transformative renewal? It can, only if the time frame for such a change is ample and the possibility (likelihood?) of a shorter term interlude of a reactionary and coercive regime is taken into account. The social tensions building from the pressures on the American economy and the high visibility of the dysfunctionality of American life—with its incredible capability and dismal results—are producing a boiler-room atmosphere.

Given the erosion of democratic institutions and processes that have been detailed, the multiplying crises in American life are less and less likely to be overcome by democratic means. What precisely will be the character of the political administration in the immediate years ahead, and how it will affect individual lives, are beyond prediction. It is reasonable to assume that an all-too-probable rightist regime will impose heavy burdens on the weakest groups, while proclaiming its above-class, national goals. Something along the lines of Bertram Gross' prescient work of 1980, *Friendly Fascism*, seems not at all out of the question.[13] Indeed, the legislative measures proposed by the conservative Republican congressional majority in early 1995, though not yet constituting a hardened political reality, are steps in this direction.

How long an authoritarian regime will last and how it eventually will be overturned are also beyond prediction. It cannot fail, however, to sharpen existing tensions because such a government's objective will be not to lessen social inequities but to freeze and deepen them. Such a policy can only augment the dissatisfaction and, it is hoped, increase the understanding of growing numbers of citizens. In short, these scenarios, if indeed they do occur, would signify the reemergence with mounting passion of what Fukuyama and others have claimed no longer exists—class conflict. The former editor of the *New York Times*, A. M. Rosenthal, after observing the first moves of the 104th Congress, was moved to write: "If they destroy too much of the government safety net . . . that will be not only the prescription for class struggle but the beginning of its reality."[14]

As it is, there are probably more individuals in the United States than anywhere else who have a clear and unsentimental view and understanding of the mechanics of a largely unaccountable private corporate economy. And this is despite the commercially dehydrated national informational condition. The importance of such understanding cannot be overemphasized. To be sure, most of the media, and almost all of the political leadership, endlessly enthuse over the virtues of the market while the carnage, physical and human, which is the direct outcome of market forces, is strewn across the land. And it is no less remarkable that Hollywood and New York media voices can urge the world-at-large to follow American "free flow of information" practices, while, in fact, *useful* domestic information, as we have seen, is hard to come by and substantive political discourse has shriveled.

Withal, much of this is understood by many, despite the absence of a genuine political opposition at home. The "many" is certainly not a majority, but it is not inconsequential. As for the majority, there is more than enough evidence that the public mistrusts its information sources, be they governmental or commercial. The general skepticism about the political system itself is apparent at election times, when half to two-thirds of the voters in state and local elections fail to exercise their mandate. Admittedly, these are indicators of large-scale social breakdown and political apathy, not of latent radical energies. And they foretell near-term dismal political developments. But they do not invalidate the possibility of truly radical and progressive change occurring successfully in the United States, whatever the detour ahead. It could still be *before anywhere else*. No doubt, this is a substantial qualification but it is more than mere consolation.

The expectations for the United States as a site of transformation are grounded in both the industrial and ideological spheres. In each arena, the gaps between *what is* and *what could be* are almost unspannable. Here, the focus is on the ideological scene. In this respect, it is difficult to disagree with Samir Amin's description of the present cultural condition in America: "People who are not permanent residents of the West on a day-to-day basis are always struck by the incredible saturation by the dominant media—a veritable carpet bombing of the public consciousness."[15]

Amin's assessment is incontestable, but it is not the whole reality. One can point to thousands, if not tens of thousands, of independent video- and filmmakers, small presses, regional and local theatrical groups, public-access television channels, and hundreds of dedicated workers in these installations. Equally important, there are many thousands of individual artists, performers, editors and journalists, teachers and librarians, who strive to create and produce alternate images, information, and understanding. These are not uniform or orchestrated presentations, yet they are often characterized by a skepticism and questioning of the dominant institutional perspectives.

Inside the powerful commercial television networks and cable channels and the press and publishing combines, there are also significant numbers of media workers and professionals who carry out their assigned responsibilities but retain their independent oppositional views. These are derived largely from their work experiences. The most important feature, and common denominator, underlying the views of these diverse occupational groups in the information, image, and message sector is a thoroughgoing recognition of the falsity of the nationally proclaimed condition of communication diversity and pluralism.

All of this suggests therefore, that there exists in America today a wide pool of human resources. It contains talented, knowledgable, clear-eyed individuals of integrity, who could, under still-unforeseen circumstances, easily be engaged in projects that would offer a socially expanded perspective to the nation's deepening dilemmas and crises. It will be the pressures arising from these systemic crisis points that will produce the future new socially responsive alignments, political and cultural. Whether these forces will be sufficient to make a difference in the face of the world's most powerful reactionary governing order, which still enjoys substantial popular support, cannot be foretold.[16] Also, the scope of the projects that will be undertaken in the future is difficult to fully envisage. Yet one condition is clear: many of the underlying assumptions and practices of currently structured existence must first undergo immense recasting.

What sanely organized society, to take a relatively minor media matter, would continue to produce newspapers the obscene size of so many Sunday and daily publications? Such products, e.g., the *New York* and *Los Angeles Times*, epitomize waste of natural and human resources. Relatedly, what accounts for round-the-clock television transmission? Is it because there is so much valuable material to be broadcast? Or is it a function of marketing and the advertising revenues that have to be squeezed out of every second of the day and night?

Indeed, many more far-reaching measures than changing the size of newspapers and the time allotted to television broadcasting are going to be required to deal with the fast-approaching new reality. These may well entail reviewing and modifying some unshakeable assumptions that equate freedom and liberty with corporate and individual property ownership and unaccountable self-indulgence. Over the course of human existence, opportunities have been afforded to groups and cultures, at different times, to make astonishing advances—the first neolithic settlements, the first urban centers, the early city-states of embryonic capitalist enterprise, and, some centuries later, the nation-state itself. Closer to the modern era, the Paris Commune in 1870, the Russian Revolution in 1917, the Chinese Revolution of 1949, and the Cuban Revolution in 1959—despite current efforts to disparage these events—were brilliant markers, though only that, foretelling the next momentous historical step. This will be the one that will take human existence beyond commodity relationships and its present need to "master" nature.

Some interpret the disintegration of the former Soviet Union, the ascendancy of the market in China, and the changes in Eastern Europe and elsewhere, as evidence of the reversal, and indeed, the inapplicability of the historical progression noted above. Perhaps they are. But one can also alternatively believe that the experiences of the "failed socialist states," enable the advance to occur the next time in more favorable material and ideological conditions.

This process may already be underway. Some recognize that "the collapse of the ideological enemy [communism] is forcing attention to the problems of American capitalism."[17] These problems are behind a growing popular awareness that has been in eclipse for several decades. It takes into account, for example, that the income gap between rich and poor in America "is greater in 1990 than at any time since records were first kept forty years ago," and that "The gap is so wide that the combined incomes of the richest 2.5 million Americans now nearly equals the combined incomes of the 100 million Americans with the lowest incomes."[18] So too, the gap between the information haves and have nots, and the abandonment by commercial media interests of even minimal efforts to maintain an open national dialogue, swells the ranks of potential cultural and media oppositionists.

These are some of the preconditions that make it possible to believe that the next climactic human advance could arrive, in ways still obscure and at a still-uncertain time, in the United States—the sword-carrier of world capitalism in the last years of the twentieth century. If this should indeed occur, who would, or could, intervene to stop or distort it?

Notes

1. Francis Fukuyama, *The End of History and the Last Man* (New York: The Free Press, 1992).
2. Anthony Lake, National Security Adviser to President Clinton, depends on this expression. See his verbatim remarks in *New York Times*, September 26, 1993, sec. E, p. 3. The use of the term "market democracies" makes it clear that American political leadership cannot imagine a democracy without unequal incomes and stratified social classes, the inseparable accompaniments of a market economy.
3. Thomas L. Friedman, "24 Nation Group Expands Aid Plan in Eastern Europe," *New York Times*, July 5, 1990, p. 1.
4. Jane Perlez, "Western Banks To Relieve 40% of Polish Debt," *New York Times*, March 12, 1994, p. 1.
5. John Rockwell, "The New Colossus: American Culture as Power Export," *New York Times*, January 30, 1994, sec. 2, p. 1.
6. R. Suro, "Europeans Accuse the U.S. of Balking Plans to Combat Global Warming," *New York Times*, July 10th, 1990, sec. A, p. 10.
7. R. Suro, "Bush Defends Blocking Kohl Environmental Plan." *New York Times*, July 12, 1990, sec. A, p. 14.

8. The National Information Infrastructure: Agenda for Action, NTIA, Washington, D.C., September 1993.
9. Michael Specter, "Tell Tchaikovsky the News: Russian Radio Cuts Classics," *New York Times,* February 20, 1994, p. 6.
10. "U.S. Firms Test-Surf China Central TV Airwaves," *Los Angeles Times,* February 28, 1994, sec. D, p. 3.
11. Tim Golden, "Mexico Pledging Changes, Reaches Pact with Rebels," *New York Times,* March 3, 1994, sec. A, p. 4.
12. *Le Monde Diplomatique,* Paris, January 1994.
13. Bertram Gross, *Friendly Fascism,* (New York: M. Evans & Co., 1980). A more up-to-date appraisal comes from Edward N. Luttwak of the Center for Strategic and International Studies at Georgetown University. Luttwak writes: ". . . neither the moderate left nor the moderate right even recognizes the central problem of our days: the completely unprecedented personal economic insecurity of working people, from industrial workers and white-collar clerks to medium-high managers . . . . What they want is security in the jobs they already have, precisely what unfettered markets most threaten. And that is the space that remains wide open for a modern fascist party, dedicated to the enhancement of the personal economic security of the masses of (mainly white-collar) working people." "Insecure Workers Are Fodder For Fascists," *Los Angeles Times,* June 28, 1994, sec. B, p. 7.
14. A. M. Rosenthal, "American Class Struggle," *New York Times,* March 21, 1995, sec. A, p. 15.
15. Samir Amin, "The Future of Socialism," *Monthly Review* 42, 1990, p. 10–29.
16. John Kenneth Galbraith, *The Culture of Contentment* (Boston: Houghton Mifflin, 1992).
17. Richard J. Barnett, "Reflections (on the age of globalizaton)," *New Yorker,* July 16, 1990, p. 46.
18. Stanley Meisler, "Rich-poor Gap Held Widest in 40 Years," *Los Angeles Times,* July 24, 1990, sec. A, p. 11.

INDEX